# COOK CHINESE

中国菜

# COOK CHINESE

By NANCY CHIH MA

Photographs by
YOSHIKATSU SAEKI

講談社

KODANSHA INTERNATIONAL LTD: PUBLISHERS
Tokyo,     New York & San Francisco

DISTRIBUTORS:

UNITED STATES: Kodansha International/USA, Ltd., through Harper & Row, Publishers, Inc., 10 East 53rd Street, New York, New York 10022. SOUTH AMERICA: Harper & Row, International Dept. CANADA: Fitzhenry & Whiteside Limited, 150 Lesmill Road, Don Mills, Ontario. MEXICO AND CENTRAL AMERICA: HARLA S.A. de C.V., Apartado 30–546, Mexico 4, D.F. UNITED KINGDOM: TABS, 7 Maiden Lane, London WC2. EUROPE: Boxerbooks Inc., Limmatstrasse 111, 8031 Zurich. AUSTRALIA AND NEW ZEALAND: Book Wise (Australia) Pty. Ltd., 104–8 Sussex Street, Sydney. THAILAND: Central Department Store Ltd., 306 Silom Road, Bangkok. HONG KONG AND SINGAPORE: Books for Asia Ltd., 30 Tat Chee Avenue, Kowloon; 65 Crescent Road, Singapore 15. THE FAR EAST: Japan Publications Trading Company, P.O. Box 5030, Tokyo International, Tokyo.

---

Published by Kodansha International Ltd., 2-12-21 Otowa Bunkyo-ku, Tokyo 112 and Kodansha International/USA, Ltd., 10 East 53rd Street, New York, New York 10022 and 44 Montgomery Street, San Francisco, California 94104. Copyright © 1964 by Kodansha International Ltd. All rights reserved. Printed in Japan.

LCC 65–10171
ISBN 0–87011–110–8
JBC 2377–781455–2361

First edition, 1964
Revised edition, 1970
Fourth printing, 1976

# Table of Contents

PREFACE . . . . . . . . . . . . . . . . . . . . . . . . . . . . . . .   5

    THE AUTHOR . . . . . . . . . . . . . . . . . . . . . . . . . . . .   7

    HOW TO COOK CHINESE . . . . . . . . . . . . . . . . . . . . .   9

PARTY FOOD

    PARTY MENU SUGGESTIONS  . . . . . . . . . . . . . . . . .  14

    BARBECUED GENGHIS KHAN MUTTON  . . . . . . . . . . .  16

    CANTONESE STYLE HOT-POT . . . . . . . . . . . . . . . . . .  18

    MANDARIN PANCAKE ROLLS (*also see pages 125-26*)  20

APPETIZERS

    COLD MEAT COMBINATION I . . . . . . . . . . . . . . . . .  24

    COLD MEAT COMBINATION II . . . . . . . . . . . . . . . . .  26

CHICKEN

    FRIED CHICKEN WITH SHRIMP WAFERS . . . . . . . . . .  30

    EGGS AND CHICKEN IN POTATO BASKET . . . . . . . . .  32

    STEAMED CHICKEN IN YUNNAN POT; FRIED LIMA

        BEANS . . . . . . . . . . . . . . . . . . . . . . . . . . . . . . .  34

    FRIED CHICKEN WITH CASHEW NUTS; CHICKEN

        DOUBLE-COOKED . . . . . . . . . . . . . . . . . . . . . . .  36

    STEAMED CHICKEN WITH SPINACH . . . . . . . . . . . . .  38

    TOMATO, SPINACH AND CHICKEN SALAD; FRIED

        CHICKEN WITH GREEN PEPPERS . . . . . . . . . . . . .  40

FISH

    SWEET-AND-SOUR FISH . . . . . . . . . . . . . . . . . . . . .  44

    FRIED FISH WRAPPED IN PAPER . . . . . . . . . . . . . . .  46

    STEAMED FISH WITH HAM . . . . . . . . . . . . . . . . . . .  48

CRUSTACEANS

    FRIED CRAB MEAT AND BROCCOLI . . . . . . . . . . . . .  52

    SHRIMP FRIED IN EGG BATTER; SAUTÉED PRAWNS . .  54

    SHRIMP IN TOMATO CHILI SAUCE . . . . . . . . . . . . . .  56

BEEF

    FRIED BEEF WITH GREEN PEPPERS; BRAISED BEEF . . .  60

    BEEF WITH CELERY; FRIED BEEF WITH

        CAULIFLOWER . . . . . . . . . . . . . . . . . . . . . . . . . .  62

    FRIED SLICED BEEF; BEEF, TOMATO,

        CABBAGE SALAD . . . . . . . . . . . . . . . . . . . . . . . .  64

PORK

    SWEET-AND-SOUR PORK . . . . . . . . . . . . . . . . . . . . .  68

    SWEET-AND-SOUR MEATBALLS . . . . . . . . . . . . . . . .  70

    STEWED MEATBALLS WITH CABBAGE . . . . . . . . . . .  72

    BRAISED PORK WITH EGGS; FRIED SLICED PORK

        WITH CUCUMBER . . . . . . . . . . . . . . . . . . . . . . .  74

## VEGETABLES

CUCUMBER AND MEAT SALAD; CHILLED STEAMED
   EGGPLANTS; CORN IN BATTER . . . . . . . . . . . . . . . 78
MIXED RADISH SALAD;
   BRAISED MUSHROOM WITH LETTUCE . . . . . . . . . . 80
SAUTÉ BLEND . . . . . . . . . . . . . . . . . . . . . . . . . . . . . . 82
VINEGAR SAUTÉED CABBAGE;
   SWEET-AND-SOUR VEGETABLE SALAD . . . . . . . . . . 84
BEANCURD, BEEF AND CHILI SAUCE . . . . . . . . . . . . 86

## EGG

EGG FU YUNG . . . . . . . . . . . . . . . . . . . . . . . . . . . . 90
EGG ROLL. . . . . . . . . . . . . . . . . . . . . . . . . . . . . . . . 92

## RICE AND DUMPLINGS

ASSORTED FRIED RICE; SHARK'S FIN SOUP . . . . . . . . 96
FISH CONGEE . . . . . . . . . . . . . . . . . . . . . . . . . . . . . 98
FRIED CAKE WITH TURNIP STUFFING . . . . . . . . . . . 100
SPRING ROLLS . . . . . . . . . . . . . . . . . . . . . . . . . . . 102
STEAMED DUMPLINGS (*also see page 127*) . . . . . . . 104

## SOUP

ASSORTED MEAT AND VEGETABLE SOUP . . . . . . . . . . 108
FISH BALL SOUP . . . . . . . . . . . . . . . . . . . . . . . . . . . 110
CHICKEN-SHRIMP-CHAMPIGNON-EGG SOUP . . . . . . . 112

## DESSERT

ELGHT-TREASURES RICE PUDDING . . . . . . . . . . . . . . 116
FRIED CUSTARD . . . . . . . . . . . . . . . . . . . . . . . . . . . 118
ALMOND BEANCURD . . . . . . . . . . . . . . . . . . . . . . . . 120
FRIED SWEET DUMPLINGS; FRIED PASTRY . . . . . . . . 122

## Preface

THERE was a time when, to many Westerners, Chinese cookery was epitomized by chop suey or chow mein, but those days are happily forgotten, and authentic Chinese cooking is today probably one of the most popular forms of food preparation in the world. Travel where you will—Europe, the Americas, all parts of Asia, Africa, Australia—and you will always find Chinese restaurants and Chinese cookery. There is no need to ask why, once you have tried Chinese cuisine. Its eye-appeal, its aroma, and its delicious flavors are the answer and the explanation. And it is perhaps because of this felicitous combination that adventurous cooking enthusiasts tend to feel that it is a difficult and complicated form of cookery. This is not true, as perusal of these recipes will indicate. Proper organization of equipment and ingredients, as set forth below, will dispel such ideas.

Eating, according to the Chinese, is much more than satisfying hunger. It is an aesthetic pleasure, and any Chinese meal is a social occasion, a time for relaxation, conversation, and the enjoyment of food. Whether it is a simple family meal or a gathering of guests and relatives, the sharing of these pleasures is believed to promote understanding and friendship. Even the manner in which the food is served and eaten is indicative of this. Each participant in this delightful ritual is provided with an attractive, colorful porcelain or china service consisting of a rice bowl, soup bowl and spoon, main course plate, sauce or condiment dish, dessert plate, wine cup, and, sometimes, a teacup. Chopsticks of silver, ivory, lacquer, or wood are used not only to serve one's self, but also to help one's neighbor to choice bits from the serving dishes. This serving and sharing makes for longer and happier meal hours.

An informal Chinese meal consists of four courses (not including dessert): an hors d'oeuvre or first course of three or four cold dishes, sometimes served on a lazy susan, sometimes in individual bowls, and already on the large round table when the guests sit down: one hot dish—sautéed or fried: one more hot dish, this time steamed or braised, with which rice is served; soup; and if you wish, dessert may follow. More festive occasions require more courses. Obviously, leisure is necessary for the full enjoyment of Chinese cuisine, an added reason for its popularity.

Chinese wine, *Shao Hsing*, Japanese saké, Western wines, or other pre-dinner drinks may be served with the first course along with fruit juice or soft drinks for those who prefer them. Chinese tea, favored by so many Westerners, may be served throughout the meal, or, in true Chinese fashion, may be produced after dessert is finished. From this it is apparent that the cocktail hour takes place at the table, and that most of the appetizers served at this time require some sort of dining utensils—chopsticks, if you're dexterous. However, many of the hors d'oeuvres described here may be served on skewers or toothpicks for those who prefer their preprandial snacks and drinks in the living room or patio.

The ingredients required in these recipes are, of course, indigenous to the Far East, but most of them can be obtained in the West from Chinese or Japanese food stores and restaurants which are becoming more numerous all the time. Substitutions are suggested in some recipes for your convenience. Read carefully *How to COOK CHINESE* on page 9 before you attempt Chinese cookery. It will save you time and effort.

If quantities used seem small, remember that Chinese meals consist of several courses, and that rice is always served with one of them. *Unless otherwise noted, these recipes are designed for four servings.* It is better to pre-pare an additional dish as the Chinese do rather than to double or increase recipes.

The art work and design for this book were done by Masakazu Kuwata; the striking photographs are the work of Yoshikatsu Saeki; and Lucille Evans edited the manuscript. The decorative accessories and Chinese *objets d'art* are family possessions used to enhance the pleasure in our meals.

The preparation of these recipes, alone or as a joint venture in cookery with friends, will provide you with as much pleasure as your family and guests will derive from sharing the eating of them. Happiness, in China, is always associated with good food.

*Tokyo, Japan*
*May, 1964*                     NANCY CHIH MA

## The Author

NANCY CHIH MA knew nothing about cooking twenty years ago, and, in fact, had hardly ever been in a kitchen. Now she is an internationally recognized authority on Chinese cookery; she has taught this art to thousands of women of many nationalities from all levels of society, including imperial princesses of Japan; she has written nine previous cookbooks, four in Japanese, three in English (including *Mrs. Ma's Favorite Chinese Recipes* by the same publisher) and two in French; she has amassed a great collection of recipes and has tested them all. Nancy Ma has demonstrated her skill and techniques throughout Japan, has made many trips to the U.S. for the same purpose, and during the same period has raised four children, led a busy social life, and entertained constantly. She is now the proprietress of Nancy Ma's Chinese Restaurant at the Chateau Mita Apartments in Tokyo, where she delights customers with her exquisite cuisine.

Nancy Chih Ma began her study of cookery when she moved to Tokyo and was unable to find a trained Chinese cook, so necessary for her style of entertaining. Nancy then went to Hong Kong and engaged chefs to teach her their skills. She sought out her friends and persuaded their cooks to share their knowledge with her. It was not easy because most Chinese cooks work from memory, taste, and guess. Nancy persevered and soon acquired her first collection of recipes along with a high degree of skill in producing them. After mastering the Peking style, she studied (and has included here) the cookery of other regions. During these twenty years, Nancy has returned many times to Hong Kong to enlarge her collection and to increase her skill. A Japanese magazine asked her to contribute a series of recipes, thus starting her on the way to her first book and her first classes.

The daughter of a Manchurian banker, Nancy Chih Ma was born in Harbin, Manchuria, was educated there and in Japan, and is married to Paul Ma, whose family is related to the last imperial rulers of China—the Ch'ing.

Cooking is creating, Nancy says, and a source of great satisfaction. It was to share her own pleasure and sense of achievement that she started her now famous classes. What began as a solution to a domestic problem developed into a fascinating hobby, and has now become a vital part of her way of life.

## How to COOK CHINESE

BEFORE YOU plan your first Chinese meal, fix firmly in your mind that each dish must be a finished work of art and must appeal to the eye, the nose, and the palate. If it does not, it is not true Chinese cuisine. Color, texture, and seasoning of the food are matched by carefully planned presentation in appropriate settings. It isn't necessary to possess a collection of costly Chinese ware to serve beautifully. Your own colorful bowls and platters are suitable if you follow the suggested arrangements in the photographs and make each dish as pleasing to look at as it is to eat. If you do have some Chinese service, accentuate it by using it to advantage. So many kinds of attractive and inexpensive Oriental bowls, cups, and plates are available now that the acquisition of a few sets is a modest investment.

Your own cooking utensils may be used. However, you may be interested in the Chinese equipment shown in the recipes. The coolie-hat pan, an all-around and indispensable item in Chinese kitchens, is rounded at the bottom (enabling the heat to reach the food more quickly and uniformly), and it is used for both cooking and frying. A deep fryer may be substituted. A steamer with a rack is another basic need. The Chinese kind, made of wood and bamboo, is always used to reheat food as well as for the usual steaming process. Other utensils are those found in any kitchen.

The correct preparation of rice and of tea are musts when you COOK CHINESE. One cup of raw rice produces two cups of cooked rice. Wash the required amount of California-type (not instant) rice several times until the water runs clear. For "dry" rice, use one cup of rice and one and a half cups of water. Soft rice requires two cups of water to one cup of rice. Boil in a covered pan over strong heat until the water is absorbed. Turn the flame low and let the rice simmer for 20 minutes. If you ever have the misfortune to scorch the rice, the disagreeable smell can be eliminated (the taste won't be affected if you discard the scorched part) by pressing a cup filled with water into the rice and replacing the lid. You may keep cooked rice in the refrigerator for one week—it makes excellent fried rice.

In China, each cup of tea is individually prepared. Put one teaspoon of tea into a Chinese teacup and pour in boiling water. Replace the lid and let stand for 3 minutes. To drink, partially remove the lid and sip through the opening. The lid will keep the leaves in the cup. Milk and sugar are never added. If you prefer to use a teapot, put in a teaspoon of leaves for each guest, pour over them an equal number of cups of boiling water, and let stand a few minutes to brew. There are many varieties of Chinese tea, most of them available in Chinese and Japanese shops and restaurants. Experiment with them and find your favorite. Among the well-known green teas are Wu I Cha, Lung Ching Cha, Mo Li

**9**

Cha, and Hsiang Pien. Popular black teas include Kee Mun, Liu An, Wu Long, and, of course, Pekoe.

Advance preparation of ingredients and assembling of equipment saves time and energy in all forms of cooking, and especially in Chinese cuisine. Preliminary steps such as soaking, washing, cutting, parboiling, and pre-deep frying should be taken first. Seasonings should be handy. All ingredients should be arranged in order of use, cut to proper size. Each dish usually contains two or more main ingredients (meat and vegetables or fish and vegetables), and these are always cut in the same manner. The methods of cutting are as follows:

Chop:      cut into very small bits
Cube:      cut into one-inch cubes
Dice:      cut into smaller-than-one-inch cubes
Flake:     grate into shavings
Grate:     grate into fine grains
Mince:     cut very fine with knife
Section:   cut into one- to two-inch lengths
Shred:     cut into thread-like strips
Slice:     cut into very thin pieces
           (abalone, however, is cut into wavy patterns)
Wedge:     cut into triangular shapes

Chinese food is usually braised, deep fried, sautéed, smoked, or steamed. *Braising* means browning in a small amount of oil, adding broth or water, covering tightly, and cooking over a low flame until the ingredients are tender. Braised dishes may be prepared in quantity, reheated, and served at a later meal. *Deep frying is* frying, either with or without batter, in plenty of oil. To *sauté* means to cook in a small amount of hot oil very briefly. To *smoke* meat or fowl, soak first in prescribed seasonings and then smoke over brown sugar or pine needles. Food is *steamed* by placing it on a rack and steaming over boiling water for the indicated amount of time.

All the recipes in this book requiring oil are based on the use of vegetable oil. Even when food becomes cold, if it has been cooked in vegetable oil it is still delicious. Peanut, soy bean, or cottonseed oil are most often used, and they should be purified first. This is done by pouring five cups of oil into a pan and adding three slices of ginger and one leek cut in three pieces. Heat the oil until the ginger and leek are browned. Remove them, and the oil is ready to use, and it has an improved flavor. A few tablespoons of sesame-seed oil may be added after purification to provide a richer taste.

A few more hints about the use of oil will prove helpful. The pan should always be well heated before the oil is put in. The oil must be heated well before ingredients are added. Ginger, leek, and garlic should be browned slightly before other ingredients are added. Deep-fry oil can be reused again and again if it is properly saved after each use: Strain the used oil through a sieve lined with cotton; keep the oil in a covered container.

A good stock is important in many Chinese dishes. Stock from a whole chicken or from beef or pork meat is best. Bones produce a less appetizing stock. Beans and certain other vegetables, or dried shrimp may also be used. The method for all is the same. Boil the ingredients in plenty of water with a stalk of leek and three slices of ginger. Cook over a low flame, uncovered, for one hour. Add a half teaspoon of monosodium glutamate. The stock should be clear. Remove meat or bones.

And now a few words about ingredients that are not commonly used in Western cookery or that may require special preparation. If fresh abalone is used, it should be cleaned with a brush and salt and steamed for 40 minutes or more, then cut in slices. If canned *abalone* is used, the No. 2 can is suggested. Fresh *bamboo shoots* are best and these should be peeled and boiled for 30 minutes. If canned ones are all you can obtain, no boiling is necessary, but the white calcium deposit should be scraped out. *Beancurd*, which is a soft custard-like paste made from soy beans, should be kept in a cool place. It spoils quickly in a warm climate. One cake equals 3/4 of a pound or two cups. Canned *bean sprouts* should be drained before using. Heads and tail should be removed from fresh ones. Oriental *cucumbers*, *eggplants*, and *green peppers* are much smaller than their Western counterparts, but these recipes indicate the proper quantities to be used. When *ham* is required, boiled ham, about four inches in diameter, is used. Because of their outstanding flavor, *dried mushrooms* are most frequently used in these recipes. They should be soaked in lukewarm water 15 to 20 minutes, and the stems should be discarded. "Onions" means round or yellow onions, and they may be substituted in slightly smaller quantities for *leeks*. The size of *potatoes* should be such that one potato equals 1/4 pound. *Snow peas* are strung, and they are cooked and served shell and all. *String beans* may be substituted. The *vermicelli* listed in the recipes is not the Italian type, but is made from green beans, and is used in hot or cold dishes and in soup. It should be dipped into boiling water briefly before using. *Agar-agar* is frequently used in place of gelatin in Chinese cookery.

Chinese cuisine uses numerous seasonings, some of which may be new to Western cooks. Listed below are the most commonly used, with brief general information about them. However, be sure to follow the exact instructions in individual recipes when using them.

*Bean paste:* A thick sweet paste made from soy beans.

*Cornstarch:* Oriental cornstarch is heavier than its Western counterpart. In using the latter, increase quantity slightly.

*Ginger:* Fresh ginger is always best. If not available, substitute 1/8 teaspoon of ground ginger for one tablespoon of fresh chopped ginger. One slice of ginger in these recipes means a thin slice about one inch in diameter. Fresh ginger can be kept from drying out by burying it in a flower pot of moist sand or loose earth. Ginger juice is extracted by grating fresh ginger and squeezing it through a cloth or a garlic squeezer.

*Leek:* The white part only is used. In this book, "stalk" means four or five inches of this white part. Round onions may be substituted in slightly smaller quantities.

*Red pepper:* Chili or cayenne pepper may be used. It is preferable to make your own by toasting chili peppers in a skillet and rolling them on a board to produce a powder.

*Red pepper oil:* Heat three tablespoons of sesame seed oil, fry three or four red peppers in it until dark, remove peppers, and use oil only. Heated sesame seed oil may also be mixed with ground or rolled red pepper.

*Sesame seed oil:* This is used to add flavor to vegetables.

*Sesame seeds:* The black or white varieties may be used unless the recipe specifies otherwise. For added flavor, they may be toasted, but be careful, as they burn easily.

*Soy sauce:* This is probably the most important seasoning in all Oriental cookery—as salt is in Western cooking. The use of Oriental soy is recommended because the Occidental variety is more concentrated and salty. If the latter is used, reduce quantity.

*Star anis:* This spice adds special flavor to duck, pork, and beef.

*Sugar:* White granulated sugar is used unless otherwise specified. Oriental sugar is not as sweet as Occidental sugar. Therefore if the latter is used, decrease quantity slightly.

*Tabasco:* This may be used in place of red pepper if preferred.

*Vinegar:* Oriental vinegar is not as strong as Western kinds, and amounts indicated in these recipes should be decreased if the latter is used.

*Wine:* Substitute sherry, cognac, dry white wine, or saké, if Chinese wine is not available.

Always cook meat or fish partially before adding soy and salt. Boiled or fried vegetables will become a brighter green if a little salt is first sprinkled into the water or oil. It is wise to mix seasonings in advance and have them in a convenient place for adding quickly to the recipe at the time indicated. Do not add sauces to cold dishes until just before serving.

With these brief general instructions in mind, you are now ready to enjoy yourself and please your family and friends when you COOK CHINESE.

筵 席

**Party Food**

# PARTY MENU SUGGESTIONS

To the novice, combining proper Chinese dishes to make a party menu may seem difficult at first, but after a few tries it will be as simple as planning a bridge luncheon or a Sunday barbecue. Listed here are several kinds of party menus to serve as guides. These are planned for ten guests. To reduce to eight servings, eliminate one dish and cut one dish in half. To serve six, eliminate two dishes and cut one in half. And remember, rice is always served at all meals!

### CHRISTMAS DINNER

Cold Meat Combination II (*page 26*)
Fried Chicken with Shrimp Wafers (*page 30*)
Fried Sliced Beef (*page 64*)
Corn in Batter (*page 78*)
Shrimp in Tomato Chili Sauce (*page 56*)
Eight-Treasures Rice Pudding (*page 116*)

### EASTER BRUNCH

Cold Meat Combination I (*page 24*)
Eggs and Chicken in Potato Basket (*page 32*)
Fried Crabmeat and Broccoli (*page 52*)
Fried Fish Wrapped in Paper (*page 46*)
Assorted Fried Rice (*page 96*)
Almond Beancurd (*page 120*)

### BIRTHDAY PARTY

Sweet-and-Sour Fish (*page 44*)
Cucumber and Meat Salad (*page 78*)
Shrimp Fried in Egg Batter (*page 54*)
Stewed Meatballs with Cabbage (*page 72*)
Fried Pastry (*page 122*)

### BUFFET SUPPER

Steamed Dumplings (*page 104*)
Sautéed Prawns (*page 54*)
Sweet-and-Sour Pork (*page 68*)
Vinegar Sautéed Cabbage (*page 84*)
Braised Beef (*page 60*)
Fried Custard (*page 120*)

### AFTERNOON TEA

Spring Rolls (*page 102*) or Steamed Dumplings (*page 104*)
Fried Sweet Dumplings (*page 122*)
Eight-Treasures Rice Pudding (*page 116*)

### DINNER PARTY

Steamed Fish with Ham (*page 48*)
Beef with Celery (*page 62*)
Chicken Double-Cooked (*page 36*)
Tomato, Spinach, and Chicken Salad (*page 40*)
Assorted Meat and Vegetable Soup (*page 108*)
Almond Beancurd (*page 120*)

筵 席

**CHINESE FEAST**

15

# BARBECUED GENGHIS KHAN MUTTON

BARBECUED Genghis Khan mutton proves that this currently popular form of cookery has a long history. Served with soup and rice, this dish provides a full dinner. For a novel sandwich, try the meat on regular or Chinese bread.

*Ingredients*
    2 lbs. mutton, cut into 1/2″ thick slices
    Marinade:  2 tbsps. wine, 1 tbsp. soy, 2 tbsps. leek, chopped fine
    1 large piece pork or lamb suet
    2 medium-size onions, cut in 1/4″ slices
    16 fresh or dried mushrooms, soaked, stems removed
    1 lb. spinach, washed and cut in 3″ lengths
    1/2 lb. spring onions, washed and cut in 3″ lengths
    Dips:  1 cup wine, 1 cup grated apple, 1 cup finely chopped leek, 1 tsp. chili pepper powder, 1 tsp. ginger root juice, 1 tsp. grated garlic, to be mixed at the table.

*Utensils and Equipment*
    Bowl, chopsticks, Genghis Khan grill (brazier or *hibachi* may be substituted)

*Method*
    Marinate mutton for 15 minutes. Heat grill over charcoal fire and grease thoroughly with suet. Place mutton slices on grill and cook until color changes and meat is tender. Cook vegetables in the same way until tender. Place the dip ingredients in separate bowls so each guest may mix his sauce to taste. Guests may also broil their own meat and vegetables. Serve and eat hot.

*Variations*
    For mutton, substitute any kind of meat, domestic or wild, fowl, or liver. Try sliced green peppers or sliced sweet potatoes in place of any of the above vegetables.

成吉斯汗烤羊肉

**BARBECUED GENGHIS KHAN MUTTON**

17

# CANTONESE STYLE HOT-POT

THIS FAMOUS Cantonese hot pot soup is a full meal—
a delicious and unusual one. It is perfect for buffet or
barbecue.

*Ingredients*
Soup stock:  In a pot 3/4 full of hot water put 3 tbsps.
wine, 1 stalk leek, chopped, 5 thin slices
ginger, 2 tsps. salt, and dash of pepper,
and bring to boil.
1/2 lb. shrimp, shelled and with black vein that runs
down back removed
1/2 lb. oysters, shelled and washed
1/2 lb. white fish fillet, cut to bite-size pieces
1/2 lb. chicken liver, cleaned and cut to bite-size pieces
1/2 lb. chicken fillet, cut to bite-size pieces
1/2 lb. beef, sliced
1/2 lb. pork, sliced
1/2 lb. beef liver, cut to bite-size pieces
1/4 lb. vermicelli
1 lb. Chinese cabbage
1/2 lb. spinach
1 lb. Chinese noodles, cooked
Condiments: wine, soy, sesame seed paste or peanut
butter, Chinese cheese (fermented beancurd), chopped leek

*Utensils and Equipment*
Mongolian hot-pot (Dutch oven on a brazier or *hibachi*
is a good substitute), bowls for condiments and bowls
for guests
*Method*
Make soup stock in hot-pot. Put condiments in separate
bowls and arrange all ingredients attractively on one or
more platters. Each guest helps himself to meats and
sea foods, cooks them in the soup until color changes,
and then adds whatever condiments he wants. The meat
and seafoods enrich the broth. Vegetables and noodles
are cooked in the same way, and the remaining broth
is served as the last course.

打边炉

CANTONESE STYLE HOT-POT

19

## MANDARIN PANCAKE ROLLS

MANDARIN pancake rolls, often referred to as the "Ma Family Sandwich," are served with a variety of delicious fillings. Guests make their own sandwiches, choosing any or all of the fillings described on pages 125–26.

*Ingredients*
    2 cups bread flour
    3/4 cup boiling water
    1/2 tbsp. sesame seed oil
    1 tbsp. sesame seed oil for brush

*Utensils and Equipment*
    Skillet, steamer, bowl, rolling pin, pastry board, chopsticks, knife, cheesecloth

*Method*
    Mix flour with chopsticks or fork, slowly pouring in boiling water to form dough. Knead for about 10 minutes and let stand for 30 minutes. Shape dough into long sausage form (*see process illustrations*), cut to form golf-ball-size pieces, and flatten with palm into 2″ diameter cakes. Apply light coat of sesame-seed oil on one with brush and pair with another pancake to form "sandwich" with oiled side in. Use rolling pin and flatten to 8″ diameter "sandwiches." Fry in flat ungreased skillet over low heat until both sides turn slightly yellow. Remove from skillet and separate into two thin pancakes. Line steamer with cheesecloth and steam pancakes for 10 minutes before serving. Fold into quarters or halves and cover with cloth until ready to serve. Keep hot. These ingredients make about 12 pancakes.
*Note:* Roll six pairs before frying process. Peel pancakes apart immediately after frying.

    Fillings for Mandarin Pancakes are many and varied. Some of the most popular fillings are listed on pages 125–26. Fillings may also be served as side dishes at lunch or dinner.

春餅

**MANDARIN PANCAKE ROLLS**

21

冷盤

**Appetizers**

## COLD MEAT COMBINATION I

THIS colorful arrangement of cold foods makes a striking dish for dinner or buffet. Its variety of ingredients offers something special for all tastes.

*Ingredients*

4 prawns, shelled, black vein removed, and sprinkled with 1 tbsp. wine
2 baby cucumbers (for green color), sliced aslant
1/4 lb. chicken breast (for white color), cooked and sliced
2–3 mushrooms (for black color), braised and sliced
2 medium-size bamboo shoots (for beige color), canned already boiled, sliced
4 slices boiled ham (for pink color)
2 cups salted jellyfish (for yellow color), shredded
6 slices canned abalone, (for tan color)
Dash of sesame seed oil
Dash of soy
Salt and ground black peppercorns, if desired
Sauce: 2 tbsps. vinegar, 3 tbsps. soy, 1 tsp. dry mustard, 2 tbsps. sesame seed oil, 1/2 tsp. monosodium glutamate

*Utensils and Equipment*

Steamer, saucepans, skillet, bowls, knives

*Method*

Place prawns in steamer and cook for 20 minutes, or until tender. Slice prawns lengthwise into 4 pieces (*see process illustration*) and sprinkle with salt. Arrange prawns in a rose shape and place in the center of the serving platter. Cook mushrooms as in recipe for braised mushrooms (page 80) and slice. Bring bamboo shoots to boil, drain, and sprinkle with sesame seed oil and soy. Wash salted jellyfish, remove any brown spots, shred, and soak in water overnight. Drain. Pour hot water briefly over shredded jellyfish to clean and wave. (Any unused portion may be used up to one week later by keeping it soaked in water.) Drain and mix with sauce. Arrange ingredients as shown in photograph. Serve cold.

**COLD MEAT COMBINATION I**

# COLD MEAT COMBINATION II

THIS colorful cold platter is a popular first course in China, and you'll know why when you've tried it. A most flexible dish, you may eliminate any of the ingredients to reduce its size, or you may add whatever cold foods your imagination conjures up.

*Ingredients*

1 medium-size cucumber, washed, cut into 5″ lengths, sliced very thin, and sprinkled with 1/4 tsp. sesame seed oil and a dash of salt.

1/2 lb. barbecued pork, sliced. Roast pork may be substituted. Red food coloring added when cooking the pork gives color to this ingredient.

2 medium-size tomotoes, washed, and sliced vertically into 4 to 6 pieces. To achieve the shape shown in the photograph, cut a deep V at the stem end of each slice and discard the stem portion. Cut each piece in half and push the cut ends together to form a tulip-like shape.

1 lb. spring chicken, prepared as follows: Clean chicken, place in bowl, add 1 stalk leek, 2 slices ginger, and 2 tbsps. wine. Steam for 30 minutes. Make a sauce of 3 tbsps. soy, 2 tbsps. sesame seed oil, 1/2 tbsp. sugar, 1 tsp. peppercorn and 1 cup juice from steamed chicken. Heat sauce and add chicken. Bring to boil, lower heat and simmer for 20 minutes or until liquid is absorbed. Cool, bone, and cut into strips.

3 eggs, hard-boiled for 10 minutes and shelled. Make a sauce of 2 tbsps. soy, 1 tsp. sesame seed oil and 2 tbsps. water. Heat sauce and simmer eggs in it for about 5 minutes, turning occasionally. Turn off heat and let eggs cool. Cut in quarters.

1/4 lb. dried mushrooms, soaked in lukewarm water for 20 minutes, stems removed. Heat 3 tbsps. oil and sauté mushrooms over high heat for 2 minutes. Add 1½ tbsps. sugar, 2 tbsps. soy, 1 tbsp. sesame seed oil and 1 cup water. Lower heat and simmer for 25 minutes or until liquid is absorbed. Slice thin.

1 cup canned abalone (about 1/2 lb.). Dip abalone in boiling water to remove black spongy edges. Slice thin and cover with sauce made of 2 tbsps. soy, 1 tbsp. wine, 1/2 tsp. sugar, 1 tsp. sesame seed oil, mixed well together.

1/4 lb. crab meat, canned, gristle removed carefully to retain shape, and sliced in halves horizontally.

1/4 lb. vermicelli, soaked in lukewarm water for 20 minutes, drained, and cut in 4″ lengths, mixed lightly with 1/4 lb. chicken, boiled and shredded. When these ingredients are placed in center of platter, pour over a sauce made by mixing well 1 tsp. mustard powder, 3 tbsps. soy, 2 tbsps. vinegar, and 1 tbsp. sesame seed oil.

*Method*

Arrange the above ingredients as shown in the photograph, garnish with chicory or your favorite green, and serve cold.

*COLD MEAT COMBINATION II*

鶏
類

*Chicken*

# FRIED CHICKEN WITH SHRIMP WAFERS

DEEP FRIED chicken with Chinese shrimp wafers and chestnuts is for special occasions. Its secret is the syrup coating on the chicken skin after the chicken is steamed and before it is deep fried.

*Ingredients*

1½–2 lbs. spring chicken, dressed
1 tsp. salt
1 tsp. black pepper
1 stalk leek or onion, chopped
3–4 slices ginger
1/2 tsp. cinnamon
2 tbsps. light corn syrup
Oil for deep frying
Chinese dried shrimp wafers for garnish, deep-fried according to instructions on package
10 cooked chestnuts or sufficient canned pineapple or canned cherries for garnish
Parsley sprigs

*Utensils and Equipment*

Steamer, bowls, deep-fryer, pastry brush

*Method*

Wash and dry chicken. Mix together salt, pepper, leek, ginger and cinnamon, and rub well inside and outside of chicken. Place chicken in bowl and steam until tender, about 30 minutes or more. Remove chicken, cool and dry. Brush light syrup thoroughly over the chicken skin. Heat oil to 360 degrees and deep fry chicken about 20 minutes or until crispy brown. Serve chicken whole, garnish with shrimp wafers and chestnuts. If you prefer, chicken may be boned and cut into bite-size pieces and served with same garnish.

Shrimp wafers may be made at home as follows: Mix well 2 cups finely minced shrimp, 2 cups cornstarch, 1½ tsps. wine, 1 tsp. sugar. Knead well like dough and form into long sausage (2″ diameter). Steam for 30 minutes. Remove, cool and wrap in wax paper, chill and let stand for one day. Slice thin and let dry for 2 or 3 days. Heat oil to 360 degrees and deep fry slices until they puff, about 1 or 2 minutes. Serve hot or cold.

炸脆皮鷄

**FRIED CHICKEN WITH SHRIMP WAFERS**

# EGGS AND CHICKEN IN POTATO BASKET

FRIED hard-boiled quail eggs and diced chicken in shredded potato baskets make an unusual and appetizing Easter brunch dish.

QUAIL EGGS

*Ingredients*

    8 quail eggs, hard boiled and shelled (substitute pullet eggs)

    3/4 cup soy (or enough to cover)

    2 tsps. flour

    Oil for deep frying

*Utensils and Equipment*

    Bowl, skillet

*Method*

    Soak shelled eggs in soy for 15 minutes, turning occasionally. Coat eggs lightly with flour. Heat oil to 340 degrees and fry eggs until golden brown. Serve in potato basket as shown in photograph.

POTATO BASKET

*Ingredients* .

    2 medium-size potatoes, peeled and shredded fine (do not wash after shredding)

    Oil for deep frying

*Utensils and Equipment*

    Deep fryer with basket, large spoon, fork

*Method*

    Fill deep-fry basket with shredded potatoes. Heat oil to 360 degrees and drop basket to fry. An oiled soup ladle may be substituted for deep fry basket. Press potatoes firmly (*see process illustration*) with back of spoon to make basket shape. Remove when golden brown. Loosen edges with fork to remove from basket.

DICED CHICKEN

*Ingredients*

    One 3/4 lb. chicken fillet, diced in 1″ cubes and sprinkled with 1 tsp. wine, 1 tsp. cornstarch

    1 clove garlic, crushed

    1/3 cup cucumbers, seeded and diced in 1/2″ cubes

    1/3 cup dried mushrooms, soaked, stems removed, and diced in 1/2″ cubes

    8 tbsps. oil

    Seasoning: 3 tbsps. soy, 1/2 tsp. sugar

    1 tsp. cornstarch mixed with 1 tsp. water

*Utensils and Equipment*

    Skillets, bowls, platter

*Method*

    Heat 6 tbsps. oil, sauté chicken over medium heat until white, and remove to platter. Heat 2 tbsps. oil, add garlic and sauté until edges brown. Discard garlic. Place cucumbers, mushrooms in skillet and mix for 1 minute. Add chicken and seasoning, stir a few times; thicken with cornstarch mixture. Serve in potato basket.

**EGGS AND CHICKEN IN POTATO BASKET**

## STEAMED CHICKEN IN YUNNAN POT

CHICKEN steamed in a Yunnan pot is an exotic addition to a buffet table. Lacking a Yunnan pot, a Dutch oven or covered casserole produces the same results.

*Ingredients*
    One 1–1½ lb. chicken, cleaned and disjointed
    2 tbsps. wine
    1 stalk leek, cut into 1/2″ pieces
    3 slices ginger
    2 tsps. salt
    1/2 cup water

*Utensils and Equipment*
    Yunnan pot, large pan
*Method*
    Place chicken pieces around the chimney of a Yunnan pot, add other ingredients, and secure lid. Place pot on top of pan containing enough water to boil for 1 hour. Steam chicken this way until tender. Remove lid and serve with stock.

## FRIED LIMA BEANS

PIQUANT seasoned sautéed lima beans can be served either as a side dish with meat or fish, or cold, as a salad.

*Ingredients*
    1 lb. lima beans, shelled
    1 tsp. salt
    2 tbsps. oil
    1 tbsp. leek, chopped
    1/4 tsp. chili pepper powder or cayenne pepper
    1/2 tsp. pepper

*Utensils and Equipment*
    Saucepan, skillet
*Method*
    Boil lima beans, remove skins, and sprinkle with salt. Heat oil and sauté leek, lima beans, chili pepper over high heat for 2 minutes, mixing well. Sprinkle with pepper. Serve hot or cold.

雲南汽鍋鶏
麻辣蚕豆

**STEAMED CHICKEN IN YUNNAN POT; FRIED LIMA BEANS**

## FRIED CHICKEN WITH CASHEW NUTS

DEEP FRIED chicken with cashew nuts is simple enough to prepare for a hurried meal and delicious enough to feature at your next party.

*Ingredients*
    1 lb. chicken, boned (or chicken fillet) and cut into 1/2″ cubes
    1 egg white, unbeaten
    1 tsp. cornstarch
    1 cup cashew nuts, blanched
    Oil for deep frying
    2 slices ginger
    1 stalk leek, cut into 1/2″ pieces
    6 tbsps. oil
    Seasoning: 1 tbsp. wine, 1 tsp. sugar, 3 tbsps. soy
    1 tsp. cornstarch, mixed with 1 tbsp. water

*Utensils and Equipment*
    Bowl, deep fryer
*Method*
    Mix chicken cubes with egg white and cornstarch. Heat oil to 320 degrees and deep fry cashew nuts, stirring constantly, until golden brown. Nuts burn easily, so as soon as color changes, remove and drain. Heat 6 tbsps. oil and sauté ginger and leek with chicken until chicken turns white. Add seasoning, stirring 2 or 3 times, and thicken with cornstarch mixture. Add fried cashew nuts, mix well, and serve hot.

## CHICKEN DOUBLE-COOKED

HERE IS a really new way to serve chicken! Double-cooked chicken is crispy golden brown, boned, and flavored by an unusual sauce. Secret ingredient: catsup!

*Ingredients*
    One 1–1½ lb. chicken, halved
    Marinade: 2 tbsps. wine, 1 tsp. salt, 2 tsps. ginger juice
    Batter: 1 egg, 3 tbsps. flour, 2 tbsps. finely chopped leek or onion
    Oil for deep frying
    Sauce: 5 tbsps. sugar, 3 tbsps. vinegar, 1 tbsp. soy, 1/2 tsp. salt, 1 tbsp. catsup, 2 tbsps. finely chopped leek
    1 tbsp. cornstarch mixed with 3/4 cup water

*Utensils and Equipment*
    Bowls, steamer, deep fryer, saucepan, platter
*Method*
    Marinate chicken for 15 minutes. Place in steamer and steam for 30 minutes or until tender. When sufficiently cool, bone, leaving meat in large pieces. Dip chicken pieces in batter which has been mixed well. Heat oil to 340 degrees and deep fry chicken until golden brown. Heat sauce ingredients in saucepan over high heat. When sauce boils, add cornstarch mixture to thicken. Slice chicken in bite-size pieces, arrange on platter, and pour sauce over before serving. Serve hot.

澆汁酥鶏

炒腰果鶏丁

**FRIED CHICKEN WITH CASHEW NUTS**

**CHICKEN DOUBLE-COOKED**

**37**

# STEAMED CHICKEN WITH SPINACH

HERE IS a Chinese version of chicken and ham, a typically American combination, that proves what subtle seasoning can do to everyday fare.

*Ingredients*
  1/2 chicken (1–1½ lbs.), dressed
  1/2 tsp. salt
  1/2 stalk leek, cut into 2″ pieces
  3 slices ginger
  5 slices boiled ham
  1/2 lb. spinach, washed and cut into 3″ lengths
  2 tbsps. oil
  1/2 tsp. salt
  1½ cups stock (from steamed chicken)
  1/2 tsp. sugar
  1 tsp. salt
  1 tbsp. wine
  2 tbsps. soy
  1 tsp. ginger root juice
  2 tsps. sesame seed oil
  Dash of black pepper
  1 tbsp. cornstarch mixed with 1 tbsp. water

*Utensils and Equipment*
  Bowl, steamer, platter
*Method*
  Place chicken in bowl and sprinkle with salt, leek, and ginger. Steam for 30 minutes. Cool and bone. Cut into about 16 pieces. Cut sliced ham into pieces slightly larger than chicken. Place on platter and top with chicken pieces. Heat oil and sauté spinach, adding salt. Add to chicken-ham arrangement. Heat stock, add sugar, salt, wine, soy, ginger juice, sesame seed oil, and pepper. Bring to boil and thicken with cornstarch mixture, stirring constantly. Pour over chicken and serve hot.

蒸火腿鶏片

*STEAMED CHICKEN
WITH SPINACH*

## TOMATO, SPINACH, AND CHICKEN SALAD

A SURPRISE in salads, chicken, spinach, and tomato, with a flavorsome dressing. This dish is equally good as an appetizer.

*Ingredients*
 1 medium tomato, peeled and shredded
 1/2 lb. spinach, boiled and cut in 2″ lengths
 1/2 lb. chicken fillet, cooked and shredded
 Sauce: 1 tsp. ginger root juice, 1 tbsp. sesame seed oil,
    1 tbsp. soy, dash of monosodium glutamate

*Utensils and Equipment*
 Bowl, saucepan, serving dish
*Method*
 Arrange vegetables and chicken on serving dish as shown in the photograph. Mix sauce and serve separately.
*Variations*
 Substitute 1 tsp. dry mustard for ginger root juice. Dissolve in water, adding drops of water while mixing.

## FRIED CHICKEN WITH GREEN PEPPERS

SHREDDED chicken with green peppers is a quick-to-fix and good-to-eat bridge luncheon dish. Serve it with flaky rice and a cold, crisp salad.

*Ingredients*
 1/2 lb. chicken fillet, shredded fine
 Marinade: 1 tsp. wine, 1 tsp. cornstarch
 8 green peppers (small), halved, seeded, and shredded
    crosswise
 Seasoning: 2 tsps. wine, 1½ tsps. salt, 1/2 tsp. sugar,
    dash of monosodium glutamate
 6 tbsps. oil

*Utensils and Equipment*
 Bowl, skillet, platter
*Method*
 Marinate shredded chicken for 5 minutes. Heat 2 tbsps. oil and sauté green peppers for 2 minutes. Remove to platter. Heat 4 tbsps. oil and sauté shredded chicken until it turns white. Add peppers and seasonings. Mix well and serve hot.
*Variations*
 Use shredded beef instead of chicken.

拌鶏絲菠菜

青椒炒鶏絲

**TOMATO, SPINACH AND
CHICKEN SALAD**

**FRIED CHICKEN WITH
GREEN PEPPERS**

**41**

魚類

*Fish*

# SWEET-AND-SOUR FISH

THIS RECIPE for sweet-and-sour fish is a new and different one for those who like to venture into new taste fields. And who doesn't?

*Ingredients*

   1½ lb. whole fish (carp or any yellow-flesh fish), cleaned and scaled

   Mixture A:  2 tbsps. wine, 2 tbsps. soy, 3 tbsps. cornstarch, 3 tbsps. flour

   Oil for deep frying

   1/3 cup carrots shredded

   1/3 cup leek or onion, shredded

   1/3 cup canned bamboo shoots, boiled, shredded

   1/3 cup dried mushrooms, soaked, stems removed, and shredded

   3 tbsps. oil

   Mixture B:  6 tbsps. sugar, 3 tbsps. vinegar, 1 tbsp. soy, 1 tbsp. tomato sauce, 1 tsp. salt

   1 tbsp. cornstarch mixed with 1/2 cup water

*Utensils and Equipment*

   Deep fryer, absorbent paper, skillet, bowls

*Method*

   Make 3 diagonal slashes on each side of fish. Rub well inside and out with Mixture A. Heat oil to 340 degrees and deep fry fish until crisp and golden brown (about 15 minutes). Remove fish to paper and drain. Flatten fish's stomach slightly to make fish stand as shown in photograph. Place in slow oven to keep warm. Heat 3 tbsps. oil and sauté carrots, bamboo shoots, and mushrooms over high heat for 2 minutes. Add Mixture B and bring to boil. Add cornstarch mixture and cook, stirring constantly, until it thickens. Pour over fish and serve hot.

糖醋全魚

**SWEET-AND-SOUR FISH**

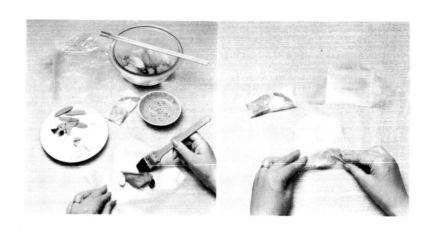

# FRIED FISH WRAPPED IN PAPER

DEEP FRIED fish wrapped in paper is so simple to prepare that even a beginner cook can produce a gourmet dish.

*Ingredients*

1/2 lb. white-flesh fish fillet, sliced in 12 pieces
1 tsp. salt
1 tbsp. wine
Dash of pepper
12 slices of ginger
12 snow peas
12 small pieces of sliced onion or leek
12 slices of mushroom
2 tsps. sesame seed oil or lard
Oil for deep frying

*Utensils and Equipment*

Twelve 6″ squares of wax paper, deep fryer, brush

*Method*

Sprinkle fish with salt, wine and pepper. Smear center of wax-paper squares with sesame-seed oil or lard and place on each one piece of fish, ginger, peas, onion, and mushroom. Fold wax paper like an envelope (*see process illustration*) and tuck in flap to secure. Heat oil to 360 degrees and place wax-paper packets in flap-side up. Deep fry for 3 minutes or until slightly brown. Remove from oil, drain, and serve hot. Paper wrapping should be broken in the center when ready to eat.

**46**

紙包魚

FRIED FISH WRAPPED IN PAPER

47

# STEAMED FISH WITH HAM

STEAMED SLICED fish with ham makes an attractive main dish for lunch or dinner and serves very well as that "extra something" for buffets.

*Ingredients*
    1/2 lb. white-meat fish fillet, cut in approximate 2″ squares
    8 slices ham, cut same as fish
    8 dried mushrooms, soaked in water, stems removed, and sliced in halves
    8 thin slices ginger root
    1 tbsp. wine
    1/2 tsp. salt
    Dash of pepper
    Dash of monosodium glutamate
    1/2 lb. spinach, lightly sautéed
    2 tsps. cornstarch

*Utensils and Equipment*
    Casserole, steamer, spatula, serving dish
*Method*
    Apply thin coat of oil to casserole and put in fish, ham, mushrooms, and ginger. Sprinkle with salt, wine, pepper, and monosodium glutamate. Place casserole in steamer and steam for 20 minutes. Loosen edges of ingredients with spatula and arrange on serving dish as shown in photograph. Garnish with spinach. Heat liquid obtained from steaming (adding water to make 1/2 cup), thicken with cornstarch to make gravy. Pour over steamed fish and serve hot.

蒸火腿魚片

**STEAMED FISH WITH HAM**

49

蝦 · 海味

Crustaceans

# FRIED CRAB MEAT AND BROCCOLI

TWO FAVORITES—crab meat and broccoli—are mated in this unusual recipe. Delicately seasoned, it is an exotic dish and a versatile one.

*Ingredients*
  2 fresh crabs or 8 oz. canned crab meat
  1 bunch broccoli, stems and flowerets separated
  3 prawns, shelled, deveined, underside split to prevent shrinking, and cut into 3 or 4 pieces, sprinkled with 1/2 tsp. cornstarch, 1 tsp. wine
  6 tbsps. oil
  Pinch of salt
  2 egg whites
  Seasoning:  1 tbsp. wine, 1 tbsp. cornstarch, 1 tsp. salt, 1/2 tsp. sugar, 1/3 cup water, mixed together

*Utensils and Equipment*
  Steamer, bowls, saucepans, skillet, platters
*Method*
  Steam fresh crabs 30 minutes or until tender and remove meat. If canned crab meat is used, remove gristle. Parboil flowerets of broccoli in salt water. Snap hard green fibers from broccoli stems, leaving light green cores. Cut into 1″ lengths and slice vertically. Heat 3 tbsps. oil and sauté stems until they turn bright green and are crisp. Remove to plate with flowerets. Heat 3 tbsps. oil and sauté prawns until color changes. Remove to platter. Beat egg whites with seasoning, add to crab meat, and bring to boil. Stir constantly and cook about 2 minutes until thick. Pour crab over broccoli and top with prawns. Serve hot.

碧玉珊瑚

**FRIED CRAB MEAT AND BROCCOLI**

## SHRIMP FRIED IN EGG BATTER

EVERYONE has a favorite way of frying shrimp. Try this deep fried shrimp with egg white—it's special!

*Ingredients*
  1/2 lb. shrimp, shelled (tails left on), black vein removed, underside split to prevent shrinking
  1/2 tsp. salt
  1 tsp. cornstarch
  Batter: 2 egg whites beaten stiff with 1/4 tsp. salt and 2 tbsps. cornstarch
  Oil for deep frying
  Half-and-half mixture of salt and pepper
  Tomato catsup

*Utensils and Equipment*
  Deep fryer, bowls, absorbent paper
*Method*
  Sprinkle shrimp with salt and cornstarch and let stand for 10 minutes. Heat oil to 320 degrees. Dip shrimp in batter and deep fry about six at a time about 2 minutes. Remove quickly and drain on paper. Shrimp should become white when cooked. Do not overcook. Serve immediately with seasonings.

## SAUTÉED PRAWNS

SAUTÉED prawns in this tasty and unusual combination will please all lovers of seafood.

*Ingredients*
  8 prawns (1½ lbs.), shelled, black vein removed, underside split to prevent shrinking, and cut into bite-size pieces
  Marinade: 1 tbsp. wine, 1/2 tsp. salt, 1 tsp. cornstarch
  8 tbsps. oil
  1/4 lb. canned bamboo shoots, boiled, sliced into same size as prawns
  1/4 lb. cucumbers, cut into sections and sliced vertically into 3 pieces
  1/2 tsp. salt
  1/2 tsp. sugar

*Utensils and Equipment*
  Bowl, skillet, platter
*Method*
  Marinate prawns and let stand 5 minutes. Heat 5 tbsps. oil and sauté prawns over high heat until color changes. Remove to platter. Heat 3 tbsps. oil and sauté bamboo shoots and cucumbers over high heat for 2 minutes. Add prawns, salt, and sugar, mixing well. Serve hot.

炒蝦片

炸高麗蝦仁

**SHRIMP FRIED IN EGG BATTER**

**SAUTÉED PRAWNS**

**55**

# SHRIMP IN TOMATO CHILI SAUCE

ANOTHER new way to deep fry shrimp and a memorable
one. The subtle tomato chili sauce is a perfect foil.

*Ingredients*
    1 lb. shrimp, shelled and black vein removed
    1 tsp. wine
    2 tsps. cornstarch
    Oil for deep frying
    2 tsps. ginger root, finely chopped
    5 tbsps. onion or leek, finely chopped
    1 tsp. red chili pepper
    3 tbsps. oil
    Sauce: 1 tsp. salt, 2 tsps. sugar, 4 tbsps. tomato catsup
    1 tbsp. cornstarch, mixed with 1/2 cup water

*Utensils and Equipment*
    Deep fryer, bowls, absorbent paper

*Method*
    Dredge shrimp with wine and cornstarch. Heat oil to
320 degrees, deep fry shrimp until tender, remove, and
drain on paper. Heat 3 tbsps. oil, sauté ginger, onion,
and chili pepper, mixing well over high heat for 2
minutes. Add shrimp and sauce, stirring constantly,
and thicken with cornstarch mixture. Remove from heat
when mixture thickens. Serve hot.

乾燒蝦仁

*SHRIMP IN TOMATO CHILI SAUCE*

**57**

牛肉類

*Beef*

# FRIED BEEF WITH GREEN PEPPERS

BEEF WITH green peppers is a zesty dish Westerners have always relished. This easy-to-prepare recipe is a treat for either family or guests.

*Ingredients*
    1/2 lb. beef, shredded
    1 tbsp. soy
    1 tsp. cornstarch
    Dash of pepper
    3 cups green peppers, seeded and cut in thin strips
    1 tsp. salt
    7 tbsps. oil
    1 tbsp. soy
    Dash of monosodium glutamate

*Utensils and Equipment*
    Bowl, skillet, platter
*Method*
    Sprinkle beef with soy, cornstarch, and pepper, and let stand for 5 minutes. Heat 3 tbsps. oil and sauté peppers over high heat for 1 minute and add salt. Remove to platter. Heat 4 tbsps. oil and sauté beef over high heat until meat changes color. Add peppers, soy, and monosodium glutamate. Cook for about 1 minute, stirring well. Serve hot. Serves two.
*Variations*
    Garnish with 1/4 cup cooked corn or shredded bamboo shoots.

**60**

# BRAISED BEEF

BRAISED BEEF makes a good cold weather casserole. Reduce cooking time and decrease water, of course, if a pressure cooker is used. Steam to reheat if prepared ahead of time.

*Ingredients*
    1 lb. beef, shank or round, cut into $1\frac{1}{2}$" cubes
    1 clove garlic, minced
    3 tbsps. oil
    2 stalks leek, cut into 2" pieces
    2 oz. ginger root, minced
    3 tbsps. wine
    3 cups water
    Dash of pepper
    2 tbsps. sugar
    1/3 cup soy
    Dash of monosodium glutamate
    2 tsps. cornstarch mixed with 4 tsps. water

*Utensils and Equipment*
    Skillet, deep pan with cover
*Method*
    Heat oil and sauté beef and garlic until beef changes color. Remove beef to deep pan and add leek, ginger root, wine, water and seasonings. Cover tightly and cook over high heat to boiling point. Turn heat low and simmer for about 1 hour, or until beef is tender. Add cornstarch mixture to thicken. Serve hot.

青椒炒牛肉絲
紅燒牛肉

**FRIED BEEF WITH GREEN PEPPERS; BRAISED BEEF**

## BEEF WITH CELERY

SAUTÉED BEEF with celery is not only a new taste, but a dish that the most calorie conscious can enjoy with no feelings of guilt.

*Ingredients*
  1/2 lb. beef, shredded
  1 tbsp. soy
  1 tsp. cornstarch
  1 lb. celery, cleaned and cut in diagonal slices 3" long
  6 tbsps. oil
  3 tbsps. soy
  1/4 tsp. monosodium glutamate

*Utensils and Equipment*
  Bowl, saucepan, skillet
*Method*
  Dredge beef with soy and cornstarch. Boil celery for one minute and drain. Heat oil and sauté beef over high heat until color changes. Add celery and other ingredients. Serve hot. Serves two.
*Variation*
  Shredded onion or cabbage may be substituted for celery.

## FRIED BEEF WITH CAULIFLOWER

AN UNUSUAL combination, sautéed beef and cauliflower is easy to prepare and should delight the dieter.

*Ingredients*
  1/2 lb. sliced beef, cut into bite-size pieces
  Marinade: 1 tbsp. wine, 1/2 tsp. salt, dash of black pepper, 1 egg white, 1 tbsp. cornstarch, mixed well together
  6 tbsps. oil
  1/2 lb. cauliflower, flowerets separated and parboiled
  Seasoning A: 1 tsp. vinegar, 1 tsp. sugar, 1 tbsp. soy
  Seasoning B: 1 tsp. salt, 1 tsp. sugar, dash of monosodium glutamate

*Utensils and Equipment*
  Bowls, skillets
*Method*
  Marinate beef for about 5 minutes. Heat 4 tbsps. oil and sauté beef over high heat until color changes. Add Seasoning A, mixing well. Cook for 2 minutes. Heat 2 tbsps. oil and sauté cauliflower over high heat for 1 minute. Add Seasoning B. Serve meat and cauliflower together. Serve hot. Serves two.

牛肉絲炒芹菜

**BEEF WITH CELERY**

菜花炒牛肉片

**FRIED BEEF WITH
CAULIFLOWER**

**63**

## FRIED SLICED BEEF

TENDERLOIN of beef, marinated and lightly sautéed, is enhanced by the addition of mushrooms and crisp snow peas.

*Ingredients*
> 1/2 lb. beef tenderloin, sliced thin and cut into bite-size pieces
> Marinade:  1 tbsp. wine, 1 tbsp. soy, 2 tsps. cornstarch
> 6 tbsps. oil
> 1/2 cup sliced mushrooms (canned or fresh)
> 1 cup snow peas, washed and strings removed (canned snow peas may be substituted)
> 3/4 tsp. salt
> Dash of monosodium glutamate

*Utensils and Equipment*
> Bowl, skillet

*Method*
> Marinate beef for about 5 minutes. Heat oil, sauté beef over high heat until color changes. Add other ingredients and cook for 2 minutes, mixing well. Serve hot. Serves two.

## BEEF, TOMATO, CABBAGE SALAD

BEEF, tomato, and cabbage salad is a dish for the diet conscious. It is a sturdy salad that makes a perfect Sunday night supper for two or a hearty salad course for four.

*Ingredients*
> 1/4 lb. beef, shredded
> Marinade:  1 tbsp. soy, 1 tbsp. wine, 1 tsp. cornstarch
> 2 tbsps. oil
> 1/2 lb. cabbage, outside leaves discarded, washed, shredded, and sprinkled with 1 tsp. salt
> 1 medium tomato, peeled, sliced, and shredded
> Sauce:  1 tsp. ginger root juice, 1½ tbsps. sesame-seed oil, 1 tbsp. soy, mixed together

*Utensils and Equipment*
> Bowls, platter, skillet

*Method*
> Marinate beef and let stand 5 minutes. Heat oil and sauté beef until color changes. Remove to platter and cool. Squeeze water from cabbage. Arrange salad on a platter as follows: cabbage on the bottom, tomatoes next, and beef on top. Pour sauce on salad before serving. Serve cold.

炒牛肉片

牛肉絲拌卷心菜

**FRIED SLICED BEEF**

**BEEF, TOMATO,
CABBAGE SALAD**

**65**

猪肉類

*Pork*

# SWEET-AND-SOUR PORK

MANY DEVOTEES of Chinese cooking tell me they date their interest from their first taste of sweet-and-sour pork. Here's an especially good version of this famous dish.

*Ingredients*
1 lb. lean pork, cut into 1/2″ thick bite-size pieces
1 tbsp. wine
1 tbsp. soy
1 egg, lightly beaten
1 tbsp. cornstarch
3 tbsps. flour
Oil for deep frying
1 small onion, quartered
3 green peppers, quartered and seeded
1 clove garlic, minced
3 slices canned pineapple, drained and quartered
3 tbsps. oil
Sauce:  1/3 cup sugar, 4 tbsps. catsup or Chinese crabapple sauce, 1 tbsp. wine, 2 tbsps. vinegar, 4 tbsps. soy, mixed well together
1 tbsp. cornstarch mixed with 1/3 cup water

*Utensils and Equipment*
 Bowls, oven-proof platter, absorbent paper, skillet, deep fryer

*Method*
Mix pork with wine, soy, egg, cornstarch, and flour. Heat oil for deep frying to 340 degrees, separate pork pieces, and deep fry until well done and crisp on edges. Remove to oven-proof platter covered with absorbent paper, and place in low oven to keep warm. Heat 3 tbsps. oil and sauté onions, green peppers, and garlic over high heat for 2 minutes, mixing well. Add sauce and bring to boiling point. Thicken with cornstarch mixture, stirring constantly. Add fried pork and pineapple, mix well, and serve hot.

**SWEET-AND-SOUR PORK**

# SWEET-AND-SOUR MEATBALLS

SWEET-AND-SOUR meatballs is a versatile dish. Serve it for lunch, dinner, or as an attractive buffet side dish.

*Ingredients*
 1 lb. ground pork, mixed with 1 tbsp. chopped leek
 1/2 tsp. ginger root juice
 1/2 tsp. garlic, minced
 1 egg
 1 tbsp. wine
 1 tsp. salt
 1 tbsp. soy
 1 tbsp. sesame seed oil
 2 tbsps. cornstarch
 2 tbsps. flour
 Oil for deep frying
 20 Brussels sprouts
 Dash of salt
 Sauce:  5 tbsps. sugar, 4 tbsps. vinegar, 3 tbsps. soy,
          1/2 tsp. salt, 1 tsp. wine, 1/3 cup broth (or
          water)
 $1\frac{1}{2}$ tbsps. cornstarch mixed with $1\frac{1}{2}$ cups water

*Utensils and Equipment*
 Deep fryer, saucepans, bowl, tablespoons
*Method*
 Mix first eleven ingredients well and use tablespoons to shape into small balls (*see process illustration*). Heat oil to 360 degrees and deep fry meatballs over medium heat until golden brown. Boil Brussels sprouts with dash of salt for about 8 minutes or until tender and drain. Put sauce ingredients in pan and boil, stirring constantly. Thicken with cornstarch mixture. Add fried meatballs and Brussels sprouts when sauce has thickened. Serve hot.

**70**

糖醋肉丸

**SWEET-AND-SOUR MEATBALLS**

**71**

# STEWED MEATBALLS WITH CABBAGE

GROUND PORK balls stewed with cabbage and spicy seasoning make an unusual casserole that tempts the most jaded palate.

*Ingredients*

    1 lb. pork, ground fine
    1 stalk leek, chopped
    1 tsp. ginger root, minced
    3/4 cup bamboo shoots, chopped
    1 egg lightly beaten
    1 tbsp. wine
    1 tsp. salt
    1 tbsp. cornstarch mixed with 2 tbsps. water
    1/3 cup oil
    2 lbs. round or Chinese cabbage, washed, leaves separated (outside leaves discarded), and cut coarsely
    2 tbsps. soy
    2 cups water
    3 tbsps. wine

*Utensils and Equipment*

    Chopsticks, bowl, large deep skillet, platter

*Method*

Using chopsticks (or fork), mix pork well with leek, ginger root, bamboo shoots, egg, wine, and salt. Divide into 4 equal portions. Wet hands with cornstarch batter and shape mixture into 4 balls. Heat oil to 340 degrees and sauté meatballs until golden brown. Remove to platter. Use same oil to sauté cabbage for about 2 minutes. Spread cabbage over bottom of skillet, place meatballs on top, add soy, water, and wine, cover and simmer over low heat for about 1 hour. Serve hot.

*Note:* Bamboo shoots may be omitted.

**STEWED MEATBALLS WITH CABBAGE**

## BRAISED PORK WITH EGGS

BRAISED fresh bacon with eggs makes a new kind of brunch dish. It's good too for Sunday supper.

*Ingredients*
- 1½ lbs. fresh bacon, cut into 1½″ cubes
- 3 tbsps. oil
- 3 tbsps. wine
- 6 tbsps. soy
- 1 tbsp. sugar
- 1 stalk leek, cut into 1½″ lengths
- 6 slices ginger root
- 1/2 lb. bamboo shoots, boiled and cubed
- 1½ cups water
- 4 eggs, hard-boiled and shelled

*Utensils and Equipment*
Skillet, deep pan, serving dish

*Method*
Heat oil and sauté fresh bacon over medium heat until color changes. Add wine and soy and continue to cook over medium heat until meat absorbs sauce (about 5 minutes). Remove to deep pan. Add other ingredients except eggs. Cover pan tightly and cook over low heat for 1 hour. Add whole boiled eggs and simmer for 30 minutes. Remove to serving dish and cut eggs in half. Add stock from pan and serve hot.

## FRIED SLICED PORK WITH CUCUMBER

WITH SAUTÉED sliced pork and cucumbers, a very easy-to-prepare dish, even the beginner can pose as a chef.

*Ingredients*
- 1/4 lb. sliced pork, cut in bite-size pieces
- Marinade: 1 tsp. wine, 2 tsps. soy, 1 tsp. cornstarch
- 2 cups baby cucumbers, sliced diagonally (large cucumbers may be scored or peeled)
- 3 tbsps. oil
- 1 tbsp. soy
- 1/2 tsp. sugar
- Dash of monosodium glutamate

*Utensils and Equipment*
Bowl, skillet

*Method*
Marinate pork and let stand for 5 minutes. Heat oil and sauté pork over high heat until color changes. Add other ingredients, mix well, and cook for about 1 minute. Serve hot. Serves two.

紅燒肉

**BRAISED PORK WITH EGGS**

肉片炒黃瓜

**FRIED SLICED PORK
WITH CUCUMBER**

**75**

蔬菜類

Vegetables

## CUCUMBER AND MEAT SALAD

CUCUMBER and meat salad is the answer for a hot day dinner.

*Ingredients*

1/2 lb. cucumbers, washed, lightly rubbed with salt, sliced diagonally and shredded

1/2 lb. boiled ham, shredded

2 eggs, beaten

1/4 lb. cooked chicken, shredded

Sauce: 3 tbsps. soy, 1 tsp. dry mustard, 3 tbsps. vinegar, 2 tbsps. sesame seed oil, dash of monosodium glutamate

*Utensils and Equipment*

Skillet, platter, bowl

*Method*

Apply thin coat of oil to skillet, fry eggs into thin sheets, and shred. Arrange ingredients on platter as shown in the photo and chill. Mix sauce at table and stir well. Pour sauce over salad and toss before serving.

## CHILLED STEAMED EGGPLANTS

CHILLED steamed eggplant can be served as a vegetable or a salad.

*Ingredients*

1 lb. small eggplants

1 tbsp. sesame paste diluted with 1 tbsp. water

1 tbsp. soy

1 tbsp. vinegar

1/2 tsp. sugar

*Utensils and Equipment*

Bowls, steamer

*Method*

Make lengthwise slits on eggplant and place in cold water to prevent discoloration. Steam eggplant until tender, about 15 or 20 minutes. Remove and chill. Mix sesame paste-water mixture with other ingredients to make sauce and chill. Pour sauce over eggplant before serving.

## CORN IN BATTER

DEEP FRIED corn in batter, crisp and golden, will add tang to any meal, and is particularly good with leftovers.

*Ingredients*

$2\frac{1}{2}$ ears corn, fresh

Batter: 2 eggs, 3/4 tsp. salt, dash of pepper, 1/3 cup flour, dash of monosodium glutamate

Oil for deep frying

*Utensils and Equipment*

Saucepan, bowl, deep fryer, absorbent paper

*Method*

Strip corn, leaving a few husks. Cover with water and boil until tender. Cut off kernels (about $2\frac{1}{2}$ cups). Mix batter ingredients together and add corn. Mix well. Heat oil to 360 degrees and drop in batter, 1 tbsp. at a time. Deep fry until golden brown. Drain on absorbent paper. Serve hot.

**78**

涼拌茄子　炸苞米塊　拌肉絲黃瓜

CHILLED STEAMED
EGGPLANTS

CORN IN BATTER

CUCUMBER AND
MEAT SALAD

## MIXED RADISH SALAD

A RADISH-and-ham salad, which is simple to make and so delicious, goes well with rich beef or pork dishes.

*Ingredients*
2 cups radishes, peeled and shredded
1 tbsp. leek, shredded
1/4 cup boiled ham, shredded
Sauce: 1 tbsp. soy, 2 tbsps. vinegar, 2 tbsps. sugar,
        1 tbsp. sesame seed oil, mixed together well

*Utensils and Equipment*
Salad bowl, mixing bowl
*Method*
Mix all ingredients in salad bowl. Pour sauce over salad before serving.

## BRAISED MUSHROOM WITH LETTUCE

BRAISED mushrooms and lettuce is the answer to "what new kind of vegetable course is there?" Serving this special treat will assure your reputation as a gourmet.

*Ingredients*
1 lb. lettuce, separated, washed, and drained
4 tbsps. oil
1½ tsps. salt
1 tsp. wine
Dash of monosodium glutamate
1/4 lb. fresh mushrooms (small), washed with salt water
    and stems removed, OR
24 dried mushrooms (small), soaked in lukewarm water
    for 20 minutes and stems removed
3 tbsps. oil
2 tbsps. soy
1½ tsps. sugar
1 tbsp. wine
1 tbsp. sesame seed oil
3/4 cup broth or water
2 tsps. cornstarch mixed with 2 tbsps. water

*Utensils and Equipment*
Bowl, skillet, platter, saucepan with lid
*Method*
Heat 4 tbsps. oil and sauté lettuce over high heat for 2 minutes. Sprinkle with salt, wine, and monosodium glutamate and remove to platter. Heat 3 tbsps. oil and sauté mushrooms over medium heat for 3 minutes. Add soy, sugar, wine, sesame seed oil, and broth. Cover pan, lower heat, and simmer 25 minutes. Add cornstarch mixture to thicken. Pour mushroom mixture over lettuce and serve hot.

拌蘿蔔絲

**MIXED RADISH SALAD**

燴冬菇

**BRAISED MUSHROOM
WITH LETTUCE**

# SAUTÉ BLEND

TRANSLATED, the name of this recipe means "Eight Precious (Ingredients) Sautéed." It is a delicious dish, equally good as a main course at lunch, or as a side dish at dinner or buffet.

*Ingredients*
1/2 lb. shrimp, shelled, black vein removed
Marinade: 1 tsp. wine, 1 tsp. cornstarch, dash of pepper
1/4 lb. chicken fillet or pork, sliced thin
Marinade: 1/2 tsp. wine, 1/2 tsp. cornstarch
2 chicken livers, washed and cut in bite-size pieces
Marinade: 1/2 tsp. wine, 1/2 tsp. ginger root juice, 1/2 tsp. cornstarch
2 abalones, canned, sliced thin and cut in bite-size pieces
2 dried mushrooms, soaked, stems removed, and cut in quarters
2 slices ham (thin), cut in bite-size pieces
2 oz. snow peas, washed and strings removed
1/2 stalk leek, cleaned and cut into 1″ pieces
1 tbsp. wine
3 tbsps. soy
2 tsps. sugar
9 tbsps. oil

*Utensils and Equipment*
Bowls, skillet, platters
*Method*
Marinate separately shrimp, chicken fillet, and chicken liver in respective mixtures and let stand for 10 minutes. Heat 3 tbsps. oil and sauté shrimp until color changes. Remove to platter. Heat another 3 tbsps. oil and sauté chicken until color changes. Remove to platter. Use remaining 3 tbsps. oil to sauté chicken livers until color changes. Add abalone, mushrooms, ham, snow peas, and leek and sauté for 3 minutes over high heat. Add shrimp, chicken, wine, soy, sugar, and stir well. Serve hot.

炒八宝菜

**SAUTÉ BLEND**

# VINEGAR SAUTÉED CABBAGE

VINEGAR sautéed cabbage is a spicy way to prepare and serve a favorite vegetable.

*Ingredients*
    1 lb. cabbage, washed, cored, cut into quarters, (outer leaves discarded), and cut into 2″ triangular shapes
    1 clove garlic, crushed
    3 red peppers, each cut in three pieces and seeded
    2 tbsps. vinegar
    1 tbsp. soy
    2 tbsps. sugar
    1/2 tsp. salt
    Dash of monosodium glutamate
    4 tbsps. oil
    1 tsp. cornstarch mixed with 2 tsps. water

*Utensils and Equipment*
    Skillet
*Method*
    Heat oil, sauté garlic over high heat for 2 minutes and remove. Add cabbage and red pepper, and continue cooking, mixing constantly. Add vinegar, soy, sugar, salt, and monosodium glutamate. Before cabbage gives off juice, thicken with cornstarch batter.

# SWEET-AND-SOUR VEGETABLE SALAD

HERE IS a sweet-and-sour salad, lightly seasoned and crisply chilled, that is a good companion to fish, meat, or fowl.

*Ingredients*
    3 small cucumbers, first cut lengthwise and then into 3 pieces each
    1/2 lb. cabbage, cleaned and cut into $1\frac{1}{2}$″ squares
    5 green peppers, cut into quarters and seeded
    3 tbsps. oil
    4 tbsps. sugar
    1/2 tsp. salt
    2 tbsps. soy
    3 tbsps. vinegar
    1/4 tsp. monosodium glutamate

*Utensils and Equipment*
    Skillet, platter, bowl
*Method*
    Heat oil, sauté cucumbers, cabbage, and green peppers over high heat for 2 minutes, and add seasonings. Mix well and allow seasonings to soak in. Remove to platter or bowl and chill well in refrigerator before serving.

糖醋卷小菜

糖醋素菜

**SWEET-AND-SOUR
VEGETABLE SALAD**

**VINEGAR SAUTEED CABBAGE**

# BEANCURD, BEEF AND CHILI SAUCE

As more Westerners adopt the Oriental favorite, bean-curd, the demand for recipes grows. Try this one—bean-curd with minced beef.

*Ingredients*
    2 loaves beancurd, boiled, drained, and diced ($1\frac{1}{2}$ lbs.)
    1/4 lb. ground beef
    1/3 cup chopped onion,
    1/2 tsp. grated garlic,
    4 tbsps. oil
    3 chili peppers, chopped
    3 tbsps. soy
    1/2 tsp. sugar
    2 tsps. cornstarch mixed with 2 tbsps. water

*Utensils and Equipment*
    Skillet, bowl

*Method*
    Heat oil, sauté onion and garlic, adding beef, and cook for about 4 minutes. Add bean curd, pepper, soy, and sugar, and bring to a boil. Thicken with cornstarch paste, mixing well. Serve hot.

麻婆豆腐

**BEANCURD, BEEF AND CHILI SAUCE**

蛋　類

**Egg**

# EGG FU YUNG

EGG FU YUNG has long been a favorite dish among Westerners because it is simple to prepare, delicious to eat, and good to look at.

*Ingredients*
>    1/2 lb. canned crab meat, gristle removed, separated into bits
>    1 tsp. ginger root, minced
>    1 tbsp. wine
>    6 eggs
>    1/2 tsp. salt
>    9 tbsps. oil
>    2 dried mushrooms, soaked, stems removed, and shredded
>    1/8 lb. bamboo shoots, boiled and shredded
>    1/2 stalk leek or onion, shredded
>    3/4 cup soup stock
>    2 tbsps. soy
>    2 tbsps. green peas, canned or boiled
>    1 tbsp. cornstarch mixed with 1 tbsp. water

*Utensils and Equipment*
>    Bowls, skillets, spatula, egg beater

*Method*
>    Mix crab meat with ginger root and wine. Beat eggs lightly, add crab meat and salt. Heat 7 tbsps. oil in skillet and pour in egg-crab meat mixture. Use 9″ skillet if one large omelet is desired or smaller skillet for individual omelets. Use spatula to draw solidified portions to one side, tilt skillet to let uncooked part run to sides. Use medium heat. Repeat process until omelet sets. Fry on both sides. Heat remaining 2 tbsps. oil and sauté mushrooms, bamboo shoots, and leek over high heat for 1 minute. Add green peas, soy, and soup stock to make sauce. Bring to boiling point and add cornstarch mixture to thicken. Pour sauce over omelet and serve hot.

芙
蓉
蟹

*EGG FU YUNG*

# EGG ROLL

EGG ROLL, an unusual combination of flavors, is a useful dish—equally welcome as a cocktail snack or a dinner side dish.

*Ingredients*
  1/2 lb. ground beef or pork
  2 tsps. wine
  2 tsps. soy
  1 tsp. ginger root juice
  1/4 tsp. salt
  2 tsps. cornstarch
  3 tbsps. chopped onion,
  2 tbsps. oil
  3 eggs, beaten and sprinkled with dash of salt
  3 tbsps. flour mixed with 3 tbsps. water
  Oil for deep frying

*Utensils and Equipment*
  Bowls, deep fryer, 9″ skillet, knife

*Method*
  Mix ground meat well with wine, soy, ginger root juice, salt, cornstarch, and onion. Divide into 5 equal portions and flatten to pancake shape. Apply a thin coating of oil on 9″ skillet and heat. Pour in 1/5 of egg mixture—enough to make thin pancake covering skillet bottom. As soon as egg sets, remove from heat to cool slightly. Using fingers peel egg sheet from skillet and set aside. Repeat until all five sheets are finished. Place one portion of ground meat mixture (*see process illustration*) on each egg sheet and roll from outside in jelly roll style. Seal with flour-and-water mixture. Cut diagonally into 6 pieces. Heat oil to 340 degrees and deep fry. Serve with salt and ground black peppercorns, catsup, or your favorite condiment.

炸蛋卷

**EGG ROLL**

93

飯・麵類

*Rice and Dumplings*

## ASSORTED FRIED RICE

COMBINING leftover rice with this group of ingredients produces a delectable Sunday brunch.

*Ingredients*
- 2 eggs, beaten and mixed with 1/4 tsp. salt and dash of monosodium glutamate
- 1 tbsp. oil
- 1/4 lb. shrimp, shelled, black vein removed, and boiled
- 1/4 lb. chicken fillet, diced
- 1/4 lb. boiled ham, diced
- 1/4 lb. canned bamboo shoots, boiled, diced
- 2 dried mushrooms, soaked, stems removed, and quartered
- 2 tbsps. oil
- 2 stalks leek, shredded
- 4 cups rice, cooked and cooled
- 5 tbsps. oil
- 1/4 lb. green peas, canned or boiled for 5 minutes, drained
- 1 tsp. salt

*Utensils and Equipment*
Skillet, wooden spoon

*Method*
Heat 1 tbsp. oil, scramble egg mixture, and set aside. Heat 2 tbsps. oil, sauté shrimp, chicken, ham, bamboo shoots, and mushrooms over high heat for 1 minute, and set aside. Heat 5 tbsps. oil, sauté leek for 1 minute and add rice. Turn heat to medium and use wooden spoon to separate rice chunks. When rice is separated, add other ingredients. Mix well. Serve hot.

## SHARK'S FIN SOUP

SHARK'S FIN soup is served in China as a special honor to guests and is considered a delicious dish, well worth the elaborate preparation required.

*Ingredients*
- 1/4 lb. refined shark's fin
- 1/6 tsp. soda
- 3 stalks leek or 2 onions
- 15 slices ginger
- 1½ lbs. stewing chicken
- 3/4 cup bamboo shoots, shredded
- 1/3 cup snow peas
- 1/3 cup boiled ham, shredded
- Seasoning: 3 tbsps. wine, 2 tbsps. soy, 1 tsp. salt or more to suit taste, 1/2 tsp. sugar, mixed well
- Dash of vinegar or more to suit taste

*Utensils and Equipment*
Large saucepans, platter, bowl

*Method*
Boil shark's fin in ample water with 1 stalk leek, 5 slices ginger, and soda. Bring to boiling point, remove from fire and let stand overnight. Rinse shark's fin well in cold water 3 or 4 times. Boil for an hour in plenty of water with 1 stalk leek and 5 slices ginger. Rinse well and drain. Boil chicken for 1½ hours with 1 stalk leek and 5 slices ginger. Use enough water to produce 8 cups of broth. Remove chicken; bone and shred. Boil shark's fin again in chicken broth for 30 minutes. Add chicken, bamboo shoots, ham, snow peas, vinegar, and seasonings. Serve hot.

ASSORTED FRIED RICE; SHARK'S FIN SOUP

## FISH CONGEE

THIS FISH congee is simple to prepare, delicious to eat, and a new taste treat on "fish day."

*Ingredients*
    1/2 cup rice, washed and drained
    5 cups water
    6 oz. white-flesh fish fillet, cut into 1″ squares
    1/3 cup dried mushrooms, soaked in water, stems removed, and diced
    2 tsps. wine
    1 tsp. salt
    Dash of pepper
    Dash of monosodium glutamate

*Utensils and Equipment*
    Rice cooker, bowl

*Method*
    Put rice and water in cooker and cook over high heat to boiling point. Lower heat and let simmer for 40 minutes until a gruel is formed. Add fish and mushrooms, stir, and boil for 5 minutes. Add other ingredients. Stir and serve.

*Variations*
    Sprinkle with finely chopped leek or chopped cooked shrimp.

**FISH CONGEE**

# FRIED CAKE WITH TURNIP STUFFING

THESE delectable cakes make an ideal snack.

*Ingredients*

Dough A: 1½ cups flour, 6 tbsps. lard

Dough B: 3 cups flour, 1/2 cup water, 1 tbsp. lard

1½ cups turnip, shredded and soaked in enough salt
water to cover for 30 minutes (1 tsp. salt)

2 oz. ham, chopped

1 tsp. lard

Oil for deep frying

*Utensils and Equipment*

Rolling pin, pastry board, knife, deep fryer, absorbent
paper

*Method*

Mix ingredients separately to form Dough A and
Dough B. Knead each well to make soft dough. Roll
each into long sausage form, 1½″ in diameter. Cut each
into 18 golf-ball-size pieces. Roll ball B to flat round
shape about 4″ in diameter and place ball A in center,
wrap and roll (*see process illustration*). Roll flattened
piece like jelly roll, press and then roll lengthwise.
Flatten showing layers on top and roll with rolling
pin to form round pieces 1/2″ thick and 4″ in diameter.
Squeeze soaked turnips, mix well with ham and lard to
form filling. Place 1 tbsp. of filling on center of wrapping and wrap. Heat oil for deep frying to 320 degrees,
fry until golden brown, and remove to absorbent paper.
Reheat in oven, if necessary, before serving.

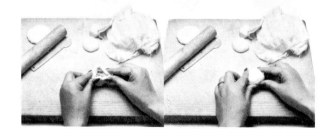

蘿蔔絲餅

**FRIED CAKE WITH
TURNIP STUFFING**

## SPRING ROLLS

SPRING ROLLS are perfect as hors d'oeuvres for the Western host.

*Ingredients—Filling*

    1/2 lb. chicken, shredded and mixed with 1 tbsp. wine, 1 tsp. cornstarch

    1 cup shrimp or crab meat, shelled, shredded and mixed with 1 tbsp. wine, 1 tsp. cornstarch

    5 tbsps. oil

    $1\frac{1}{2}$ cups boiled bamboo shoots, shredded

    3/4 cup dried mushrooms, soaked, stems removed, and shredded

    5 tbsps. oil

    1 tbsp. soy

    1/2 tsp. salt

    1 tbsp. cornstarch mixed with 3 tbsps. water

    Oil for frying

*Ingredients—Wrapping*

    1 cup flour, 3/4 cup water, 1/2 tsp. salt

*Utensils and Equipment*

    Skillets, bowls, pastry brush, 7″ frying pan, pancake turner, deep fryer

*Method—Filling*

Heat 5 tbsps. oil and sauté chicken and seafood mixtures over high heat until color changes (about 3 minutes). Remove to a bowl. Heat second 5 tbsps. oil and sauté bamboo shoots and mushrooms over high heat for about 2 minutes. Add chicken, seafood mixtures, soy and salt, and mix well. Add cornstarch mixture, stirring well to thicken. Transfer to bowl and let cool.

*Method—Wrapping*

Mix flour and water to form smooth batter and let stand for 30 minutes. Grease heated skillet slightly and use pastry brush to spread a thin 5″ pancake (*see process illustration*). As soon as batter sets, remove from skillet. Repeat process until batter is used up.

Place $1\frac{1}{2}$ tbsps. filling on the lower half of the wrappings (*see process illustrations*). Fold bottom edge up, left and right edges over, then roll. Moisten top edge with a flour-and-water mixture to seal. Heat oil to 340 degrees in deep fryer and fry rolls until golden brown and crisp.

**SPRING ROLLS**

# STEAMED DUMPLINGS

STEAMED DUMPLINGS are a delightful snack. This tasty filling, served here in Flower Wrapping, may be used with two other wrappings—Cantonese Style and Instant Wrapping—which are described on page 127.

*Ingredients—Filling*

    1 medium-size onion, chopped fine

    1 lb. ground pork

    1/2 lb. canned crab meat, gristle removed, separated into bits

    1 tbsp. wine

    1 tbsp. soy

    1 tsp. salt

    1/4 tsp. sugar

    1 tbsp. sesame seed oil

    1 tbsp. cornstarch

*Ingredients—Flower Wrapping*

    $1\frac{1}{2}$ cups sifted soft flour

    3/4 cup boiling water

    1 egg yolk, hard boiled, crumbled

    1 tbsp. spinach, boiled, chopped

    1 tbsp. boiled ham, chopped

    1 tbsp. cornstarch

*Utensils and Equipment*

    Pastry board, chopsticks, mixing bowls, rolling pin, damp cloth, cheesecloth, steamer, knife

*Method—Filling*

    Mix together all ingredients and let stand in bowl while preparing wrappings.

*Method—Flower Wrappings*

    Mix flour with boiling water, using chopsticks briskly, until cool enough to handle. Knead well, cover with damp cloth, and let stand for 20 minutes. Roll in a long sausage form and cut into 30 pieces. Flatten each piece with palm of hand and roll into thin pancake. Sprinkle cornstarch on edges and use rolling pin to flatten (*see process illustrations*) to $3\frac{1}{2}''$ diameter size. Place appropriate amount of filling on center of each pancake and wrap, leaving edges free. Place pinch of egg yolk, green spinach, and ham as garnish on mouth of wrapping. Lay cheesecloth in steamer and place dumplings on it, slightly separated. Steam for 15 minutes and serve hot.

*Note:* After steaming, remove at once to prevent sticking. Steamer rack may be brushed with oil instead of using cheesecloth. Serve with mustard or mixture of soy and vinegar, as preferred.

焼
売

**STEAMED DUMPLINGS**

**105**

湯 類　　Soup

# ASSORTED MEAT AND VEGETABLE SOUP

SHRIMP, pork, and assorted vegetables produce a hearty soup that can serve as a one-dish meal. Prepared in advance and reheated, it tastes even better.

*Ingredients*

1/4 lb. shrimp, shelled and black vein removed
2 tsps. wine
1 tsp. cornstarch
1/2 lb. ground pork
1/4 tsp. salt
1 tsp. wine
1/2 egg
Dash of pepper
1 tbsp. cornstarch
1/4 lb. spinach, washed and cut in 3″ pieces
1/4 lb. bamboo shoots, sliced
4 dried mushrooms, soaked, stems removed, and halved
1 oz. vermicelli, cut in 5″ lengths
1 lb. Chinese cabbage, washed, outside leaves discarded, cut in 4″ slices crosswise, tied with thread to form flower shape, and parboiled
5 cups broth or water
2 tsps. salt

*Utensils and Equipment*

Saucepans, bowls, teaspoon, soup pot

*Method*

Mix shrimp with wine and cornstarch and parboil until color changes. Remove shrimp, strain, and reserve stock. Mix ground pork with salt, wine, egg, pepper, and cornstarch. Roll into balls, using teaspoon as measure. Parboil meatballs for 10 minutes. Remove meatballs and reserve stock. Parboil spinach lightly and discard water. Heat broth or water and add stock from shrimp and meatballs. Add bamboo shoots, mushrooms, vermicelli, cabbage, shrimp, meatballs, spinach, and salt. Simmer until ingredients are tender. Serve hot.

ASSORTED MEAT AND VEGETABLE SOUP

什錦湯

**109**

# FISH BALL SOUP

Fish ball soup is a colorful dish that is as hearty as any Western chowder and just as filling.

*Ingredients*

12 oz. white-flesh fish fillet

5 tbsps. water

1 egg white

2 tsps. ginger root juice

1 tsp. salt

1½ tbsps. wine

1½ tbsps. cornstarch

2 tbsps. catsup

5 stalks spinach. Remove outer leaves and use a few inside leaves only (or use one stalk and cut into 2″ pieces).

Dash of salt

6 cups broth or water

2 tsps. salt

1 tbsp. wine

Dash of pepper

Dash of monosodium glutamate

*Utensils and Equipment*

Chopping block, chopper, saucepans, ladle, soup pot, bowls

*Method*

Chop fish well, adding water gradually. Mix fish thoroughly with egg white, ginger root juice, salt, wine, and cornstarch. Divide mixture equally into two bowls. Add catsup to one bowl. Form mixture into 1″ diameter balls, making 12 pink and 12 white balls. Soak in water for 10 minutes. Prepare a pot half full of boiling water and drop in balls. Boil until balls float to top. Remove balls to plate. Parboil spinach with dash of salt until tender, rinse, and drain. Bring broth to boil and add fish balls, spinach, and seasonings and bring to boil. Serve hot.

魚丸湯

FISH BALL SOUP

# CHICKEN-SHRIMP-CHAMPIGNON-EGG SOUP

CHICKEN-SHRIMP soup with champignons and quail eggs is a perfect first course for a special occasion dinner.

*Ingredients*
  6 cups soup stock (*see page 11*)
  1/4 lb. chicken fillet, sliced and sprinkled with 1 tsp. wine and 1/2 tsp. cornstarch
  1/4 lb. shrimp, shelled, black vein removed, and sprinkled with 1/2 tsp. wine, 1/2 tsp. cornstarch
  1/3 cup champignons, canned or boiled, sliced crosswise
  8 quail eggs, hard boiled and shelled (substitute pullet eggs)
  2 tsps. salt
  1 tbsp. wine
  Dash of pepper
  Dash of monosodium glutamate

*Utensils and Equipment*
  Bowls, soup pot

*Method*
  Heat soup stock, add ingredients and seasonings. Bring to boiling point. Serve hot.

四宝湯

CHICKEN-SHRIMP-CHAMPIGNON-EGG SOUP

113

甜 品 類

**Desserts**

# EIGHT-TREASURES RICE PUDDING

Eight-treasures rice pudding transforms a childhood standard dessert into this delicious confection.

## Ingredients

1½ cups glutinous rice
1½ cups water
5 tbsps. sugar
4 tbsps. shortening
1/2 lb. date paste or sweet red bean paste (*see below*)
4 tbsps. sesame paste or peanut butter
1/2 can tangerines
1/2 cup peaches, canned
1/2 cup green grapes, canned or fresh (seeded)
8 chestnuts, canned
1/3 cup raisins
1/3 cup cherries, canned
Sauce:   2 tsps. sugar, 1 tbsp. cornstarch, 1 cup water, or 1/2 cup juice from canned fruits and 1/2 cup water.

## Utensils and Equipment

Bowls, rice cooker, wax paper, steamer, knife, platter

## Method

Wash rice four times in cold water. Put 2¼ cups water and rice in rice cooker. Bring to a boil and then simmer for 20 minutes. Add sugar and stir well. Line a 7" deep bowl with wax paper cut in a circle and coated with shortening on both sides. Arrange fruits in the bowl in a pleasing design. Divide rice in 2 equal portions. Place one portion over the fruit arrangement. Cover this with layer of date or bean paste. Put remaining rice on top of paste to form final layer. Place bowl in steamer for 20 minutes. Remove, loosen edges, invert pudding on large platter, and remove paper. Boil sauce, stirring constantly, until it thickens. Pour sauce over the pudding before serving. Serve hot. Serves 6–8. Reheat by steaming.

*Note:*  Sweet red bean paste is called *tousa* in China, *an* in Japan. It can be purchased already prepared or can be made at home by boiling red beans with enough water until they become soft, adding sugar and a little salt, and mashing with 4 tbsps. sesame paste or peanut butter. Date paste is made by boiling dried dates until soft, removing skins and seeds, mashing with 4 tbsps. sesame paste or peanut butter. One small can of drained fruit cocktail may be used in place of dried fruits and nuts listed above. Syrup from the fruit cocktail may be substituted for some of the water used in making the sauce.

八宝飯

**EIGHT-TREASURES RICE PUDDING**

# FRIED CUSTARD

HERE IS an old favorite Western dessert in a new form.
Fried custard has a surprisingly delicate flavor.

*Ingredients*
    3 egg yolks
    1 cup water
    1/2 cup flour
    1 tbsp. cornstarch
    1 tbsp. sugar
    1 tsp. almond or banana extract
    Oil for deep frying
    3 tbsps. cornstarch
    3 tbsps. sesame seeds, toasted and ground (optional)
    3 tbsps. sugar

*Utensils and Equipment*
    Saucepan, platter, deep fryer

*Method*
Mix thoroughly egg yolks, water, flour, cornstarch, sugar, and almond or banana extract in saucepan and cook over medium heat, stirring constantly until mixture becomes firm. Remove to platter (platter should be sprinkled with cornstarch to prevent sticking), flatten and mold into square shape 1/2″ thick with hands, sprinkle with cornstarch and cool. When cool, cut into 3″ × 1″ strips. Heat oil for deep frying to 360 degrees and fry strips until golden brown. Mix sesame seeds and sugar and garnish fried strips. Serve hot.

FRIED CUSTARD

119

# ALMOND BEANCURD

ALMOND BEANCURD is a delightful dessert for any season
of the year.

*Ingredients*
    2 envelopes gelatin or 1 loaf agar-agar
    3 3/4 cups water
    6 tbsps. condensed milk
    1 tbsp. almond extract
    1 can (#2 size) fruit cocktail

*Utensils and Equipment*
    Saucepan, cheesecloth, bowl
*Method*
    Dissolve gelatin in water and bring to boil. Strain
    liquid through cheesecloth. Add condensed milk and
    almond extract and stir well. Pour ingredients into
    bowl, allow to set and cool in refrigerator. Cut into
    diamond-shaped bite-size pieces. Garnish with fruit
    cocktail and syrup before serving.

杏仁豆腐

**ALMOND BEANCURD**

121

# FRIED SWEET DUMPLINGS

SWEET DUMPLINGS are another delectable pastry and are simple to make. Serve them with a flourish at your next luncheon, barbecue, or dinner.

*Ingredients—Wrappings*
   1½ cups soft flour, sifted
   3 tbsps. lard or other shortening
   1/2 tsp. salt
   1/3 cup water
*Ingredients—Filling*
   2 tbsps. flour, roasted in dry pan until light yellow
   1/4 cup raisins, chopped
   3 tbsps. white sesame seeds, roasted
   1/2 cups brown sugar
   1 tbsp. water
   1 tsp. sesame seed oil
   Oil for deep frying

*Utensils and Equipment*
   Pastry board, bowl, deep-fryer, rolling pin
*Method*
   Mix flour with lard, using fingertips. When well mixed, add salt and water, and knead well. Form into 32 balls. Mix ingredients for filling. Roll dough to form thin round doily, making 32 of these. Place 1 tsp. filling in center and fold in half. Seal edges with fingertips (*see process illustration*) to form half-moon. Heat oil to 320 degrees and deep fry dumplings until golden brown. Drain and serve cold.

FRIED SWEET DUMPLINGS; FRIED PASTRY

# FRIED PASTRY

CHINESE PASTRY is noted for its light crispness and rich fillings. Fried pastry, shown here, is the perfect accompaniment for tea or coffee parties, or as the delicious finale for dinner.

*Ingredients—Wrappings*
    Dough A:   1½ cups soft flour
                    1/2 cup lard or other shortening
    Dough B:   3 cups soft flour
                    6 tbsps. lard or other shortening
                    1/2 cup hot water

*Ingredients—Filling*
    1/2 lb. sweetened bean paste or date paste (*see page 116*)
    2 tbsps. nuts, chopped
    2 cups sugar
    1/2 tsp. salt
    2 tbsps. lard or other shortening
    1 cup water
    1 egg yolk mixed with 1 tsp. water
    1 tbsp. white sesame seeds
    Oil for deep frying

*Utensils and Equipment*
    Pastry board, rolling pin, bowl, deep fryer
*Method*
    Mix A ingredients and knead into dough. Roll to form long sausage 1½″ in diameter. Cut into 28 pieces. Mix B ingredients and knead into dough. Divide into 28 pieces. Mix bean paste, nuts, sugar, salt, lard and water well to make 28 fillings. Roll B dough into doily form, place A dough in center and spread over the B dough. Roll up jelly roll style. Then curl in snail shape. Press and roll out again (*see process illustration*). Repeat procedure 2 or 3 times. Press and form flat circle. Place ball of filling in center, wrap, and press lightly with rolling pin. Apply thin coating of egg yolk-water mixture on top and sprinkle with sesame seeds. Heat oil to 320 degrees and fry pastry over medium heat until golden brown. Serve cold or hot.

# MANDARIN PANCAKE FILLINGS

FRIED PORK with spring onion is a favorite because it is both zesty and filling.

*Ingredients*

   1/4 lb. pork, shredded
   2 tbsps. soy
   1 tbsp. wine
   1 tsp. cornstarch
   1 lb. spring onions (or chives), washed and cut in 2″ lengths
   5 tbsps. oil
   1/2 tsp. salt

*Utensils and Equipment*

   Skillet, bowl

*Method*

   Mix pork with soy, wine, and cornstarch. Heat oil and sauté pork. Add onions and salt and mix well. Remove from heat before onions give off juice. Serve hot.

SHRIMP and green peas provide an interesting variation.

*Ingredients*

   1/2 lb. shrimp, shelled, black vein removed, and sprinkled with
     1 tsp. wine and 2 tsps. cornstarch
   6 tbsps. oil
   1 tsp. sugar
   1½ tsps. salt
   1 tbsp. wine
   4 tbsps. green peas, canned or boiled (optional)

*Utensils and Equipment*

   Skillet, bowl

*Method*

   Heat oil and sauté shrimp over strong heat until color changes. Add other ingredients. Mix well and serve hot.

SAUTÉED vermicelli is unusual and delicious.

*Ingredients*

   1/4 lb. vermicelli, soaked in lukewarm water for 20 minutes, drained and cut in 5″ lengths
   3 tbsps. oil
   2 tbsps. soy
   1/2 cup water

*Utensils and Equipment*

   Skillet

*Method*

   Heat oil and sauté vermicelli a few minutes. Lower heat, add soy and water. Simmer until liquid is absorbed. Serve hot.

BEEF WITH bamboo shoots is a most substantial filling.

*Ingredients*

   1/2 lb. beef, shredded
   Marinade: 1 tbsp. soy, 1 tsp. wine, 1 tsp. cornstarch
   1/2 lb. bamboo shoots, canned already boiled, cut into strips
   6 tbsps. oil
   2 tbsps. soy
   1 tsp. sugar
   Dash of monosodium glutamate

*Utensils and Equipment*

   Bowl, skillet

*Method*

   Marinate shredded beef and let stand for 10 minutes. Heat oil and sauté beef until color changes. Add bamboo shoots, soy, sugar, and glutamate, stirring well. Serve hot.

FRIED BEAN sprouts provide another "different" taste treat.

*Ingredients*

 1/2 lb. bean sprouts, heads and tails removed, washed and drained
 3 tbsps. oil
 1 tbsp. wine
 1/2 tsp. salt
 Dash of monosodium glutamate

*Utensils and Equipment*

 Skillet

*Method*

 Heat oil and sauté bean sprouts over high flame. Add seasonings, stir constantly, and remove from heat before bean sprouts dry out.

SHREDDED potatoes are an unusual and hearty filling for Mandarin Pancakes.

*Ingredients*

 2 medium-size potatoes, shredded
 Oil for deep frying
 Dash of salt

*Utensils and Equipment*

 Bowl, deep fryer, cheesecloth, chopsticks

*Method*

 Soak shredded potatoes in water for 10 minutes, drain, and dry with cheesecloth. Heat oil and deep-fry 1/4 of potatoes at a time until they turn light brown. Stir to prevent potatoes from sticking together. Sprinkle with salt while still hot.

MARINATED strips of pork are still another delicious filling.

*Ingredients*

 1 lb. lean pork, cut in long strips, 2″ thick, 2″ wide
 Marinade:  6 tbsps. soy, 1 stalk leek chopped fine, 4 thin slices ginger, 2 tbsps. wine, 1 clove garlic crushed

*Utensils and Equipment*

 Bowl

*Method*

 Soak pork in marinade for one half day or overnight. Heat oven to 350 degrees, grease rack with 1 tbsp. oil, place pork strips on rack, and roast for 35 minutes. Turn strips once halfway through roasting process. Remove pork from oven, slice, and serve cold.

*Variation*

 Deep fry marinated pork instead of roasting.

THIS scrambled egg filling is especially good for Sunday breakfasts.

*Ingredients*

 3 eggs
 $1\frac{1}{2}$ tsps. salt
 2 tbsps. ham, chopped
 3 tbsps. oil

*Utensils and Equipment*

 Bowl, skillet, egg beater

*Method*

 Beat eggs, add salt and chopped ham. Heat oil, pour in egg mixture, and cook, stirring constantly for 2 minutes. Serve hot.

# WRAPPINGS FOR STEAMED DUMPLINGS

## CANTONESE STYLE

*Ingredients*
   1 cup soft flour
   1 egg white, lightly beaten
   Few drops water
   30 green peas, canned or boiled

*Utensils and Equipment*
   Pastry board, rolling pin, one 3″ wide strip of cardboard, one
   3″ square piece of cardboard; cheesecloth, steamer, knife

*Method*
   Mix flour with egg white. Knead into soft dough and let stand
for 20 minutes. Roll dough very thin. Using cardboard strip as
pattern, cut dough into strips. Then, using cardboard square as
pattern, cut strips into thirty 3″ square sheets. Place 1 tbsp. of
filling (*see page 104*) on center of wrapping, pull four corners
together to wrap, squeeze waist, and place one green pea as
garnish on top (*see process illustration*). Line steamer with
cheesecloth and place dumplings on it, lightly separated. Steam
for 12 minutes.
   *Note:* After steaming, remove at once to prevent sticking.
Steamer rack may be brushed with oil instead of using cheesecloth. Serve with mustard or mixture of soy and vinegar, as
preferred.

## INSTANT STYLE

*Ingredients*
   1 cup soft flour
   1 cup cornstarch
   Water to spray
   30 green peas, canned or boiled

*Utensils and Equipment*
   Water sprayer, cheesecloth, steamer

*Method*
   Take 1 tbsp. filling (*see page 104*) and form into shape similar to
Cantonese dumplings. Make 30 such shapes. Roll this shape in
cornstarch, spray with water, roll in flour and spray with
water again. Repeat process 3 or 4 times to form coating. Top
with one green pea. Line steamer with cheesecloth, place dumplings on it, and steam 14 minutes.
   *Note:* After steaming, remove at once to prevent sticking.
Steamer rack may be brushed with oil instead of using cheesecloth. Serve with mustard or mixture of soy and vinegar, as
preferred.